ABUNDANCE

BESTSELLERS BY DEEPAK CHOPRA

Ageless Body, Timeless Mind

The Book of Secrets

Buddha: A Story of Enlightenment

Grow Younger, Live Longer (with coauthor David Simon)

The Healing Self (with coauthor Rudolph E. Tanzi, PhD)

How to Know God

Jesus: A Story of Enlightenment

Life After Death

Metahuman

Muhammad: A Story of the Last Prophet

The Path to Love

Peace Is the Way

Perfect Health

Quantum Healing

Radical Beauty (with coauthor Kimberly Snyder, CN)

Reinventing the Body, Resurrecting the Soul

The Return of Merlin

The Seven Spiritual Laws of Success

The Shadow Effect
(with coauthors Debbie Ford and Marianne Williamson)

Spiritual Solutions

Super Brain (with coauthor Rudolph E. Tanzi, PhD)

For Children

On My Way to a Happy Life (with coauthor Kristina Tracy; illustrated by Rosemary Woods)

You with the Stars in Your Eyes (illustrated by Dave Zaboski)

Deepak Chopra Imprint

Infinite Potential by Lothar Schäfer

Science Set Free by Rupert Sheldrake

Supernormal: Science, Yoga, and the Evidence for Extraordinary Psychic Abilities by Dean Radin

The Generosity Network by Jennifer McCrea, Jeffrey Walker, and Karl Weber

ABUNDANCE

The Inner Path to Wealth

DEEPAK CHOPRA, MD

HARMONY BOOKS

NEW YORK

To all who envision infinite abundance

Copyright © 2022 by Deepak Chopra

All rights reserved.
Published in the United States by Harmony Books,
an imprint of Random House, a division
of Penguin Random House LLC, New York.
harmonybooks.com

Harmony Books is a registered trademark, and the Circle colophon
is a trademark of Penguin Random House LLC.

Library of Congress Cataloging-in-Publication Data is available upon request.

ISBN 978-0-593-23379-5
Ebook ISBN 978-0-593-23380-1

Printed in the United States of America

Jacket design by Jaya Miceli
Jacket art by Gareeba Singh Tekam/Must Art Gallery

10 9 8 7 6 5 4 3 2 1

First Edition

CONTENTS

PART THREE

THE GIFTS OF CREATIVE INTELLIGENCE 79

ABUNDANCE AND THE INNER PATH

There are many books on how to make money, but this one is unique, I believe, by unfolding an inner path to abundance. I want the reader to discover that abundance is a state of awareness. Consciousness is infinite; therefore, it has infinite gifts to offer. This is an ancient truth that lies at the heart of the Yoga system in India. Far more than the exercises taught in yoga class (they are not part of this book), the truths of Yoga apply to every kind of fulfillment in life, including material fulfillment or wealth. *Yoga* is a magnificent word, and what lies behind its meaning is an even more magnificent vision. In Sanskrit the word *Yoga* means to join or unite. The English word *yoke* is derived from it, but where *yoke* brings to mind the image of a medieval cart drawn by a yoke of oxen, Yoga illuminates an entirely new reality. In this reality the things we normally think to keep separate are united.

The two biggest things we keep separate are the two worlds each of us inhabits. One world is "out there," the physical world of things and other people. The other is the world "in here," where the mind is constantly active, producing thoughts and sensations. The purpose of Yoga is to bring these two worlds together. If you can do that, you will be happy and successful.

Yoga emerged from the ancient Vedic culture that has guided Indian life for centuries, and money isn't excluded, certainly not on spiritual grounds. *Artha* is set out as the first attainment in life, and *Artha* in

Sanskrit means "wealth." By following the principles of Yoga, you will lead the life you were meant to live, one of sustainability, abundance, and joy. And along the way the money to support this life will come to you.

That gives you some idea why the vision of Yoga is so magnificent. At a deeper level, Yoga is about enlightenment. But for the purposes of this book, achieving happiness and success is good enough, a worthy aim that Yoga can achieve much more simply, quickly, and painlessly than you probably imagine.

Given the hard realities, particularly in these troubled times, most people would be skeptical about "the money will come" part of this promise. Money is the chief worry that pollsters find in people's lives. Far from being supplied automatically, money implies hard work and struggle. To survive you must have money; to thrive you need even more. Yet even in the wealthiest Western economies, according to data gathered by the Gallup Organization, only around one-third of respondents say that they are thriving.

The key to moving out of money worries isn't to work harder and gird yourself for the daily struggle until a future day when you can retire and relax with a sense of security. That day, once associated with age sixty-five, has been pushed further and further off. Many people, even with very good financial prospects, foresee working until they are somewhere between seventy and eighty. Nor is there any guarantee that retirement will bring a sense of security, much less well-being. Old age is a gamble on all fronts, but primarily health and money. If you have both, you will have achieved something truly rare, a thriving tomorrow when most people are not thriving today.

"The money will come" implies a very different approach to the whole subject of money. A shift in awareness is required, and no bigger shift can be imagined, because the two worlds—in here and out there—come together. When this happens, life flows along a hidden path. You are not ruled by the outward path of work, finances, family, relationships, duties, and demands. On the other hand, you are not ruled by inner beliefs, old conditioning, worry, whims, confusion, conflict, and the other discordant elements of the psyche. Each world is only half of reality. If you keep the two halves separate, you can't be whole. You will either be dominated by your external circumstances or your internal conflicts.

The whole point of Yoga, when it unites the two worlds of in here and out there, is to harmonize them. This can only happen in consciousness. You can only change what you are aware of. By becoming more aware, you can find the hidden path that brings together who you really are with the life you are meant to live. The money will come because being given what you truly need and desire is not left to divine Providence, good money karma, the vagaries of life, or the whims of fortune. In short, a state of awareness brings happiness and success, with money as needed for both.

Yoga is rarely attached to money, I know. In the West only one branch of Yoga is known to people—hatha yoga. This is the physical practice identified with yoga class, which is enjoying a wave of popularity unknown in the past (I have taken it up myself with unabashed enthusiasm). We won't be concerned with hatha yoga in these pages, but if you practice it or have looked into it, you know that the positions taught in hatha yoga are about bringing together a centered state of mind and body. This fits the overall vision of Yoga, bringing two things we normally keep separate into union. For the sake of clarity I will capitalize *Yoga* when referring to the larger vision, reserving lowercase *yoga* for the practices taught in yoga class.

It is true, as the saying goes, that money can't buy you happiness. But poverty can buy you misery. Equating poverty with spirituality is a huge mistake, I think. There are virtues to living with simple needs, detaching yourself from worldly demands, and reserving most of your waking hours for spiritual pursuits—not that many people, East or West, would actually choose such a life. But poverty doesn't make you rich in spirit, whether it is voluntary poverty chosen out of purity or forced poverty you can't escape.

The real purpose of life is the same for everyone. It is this: Connect with the generosity of spirit, and let it provide everything you need. Is need the same as desire? Will Yoga make all your wishes come true, showering you with wealth? Those are the wrong questions. Yoga brings inner joy, which is the only true measure of success. When we indulge in fantasies and wish fulfillment over money, we are compensating for a lack of joy.

This book is laid out so that Part One addresses the issue of money and wealth. Part Two covers all aspects of abundance. From Yoga we derive the things we most value—love, compassion, beauty, truth, creativity, and personal growth—in consciousness. The more aware you are, the better able you will be to access those things in abundance. Part Three reaches the deepest level of Yoga, where bliss-consciousness springs from the field of infinite possibilities. The focus of this part is the system of chakras, the seven levels where awareness can be fine-tuned and fully awakened.

If Yoga can bring joy here and now, what you need and what you desire will harmonize, because your whole existence will be harmonious. With such a complete vision in mind and everything to achieve, let's begin.

ABUNDANCE

PART ONE

THE YOGA OF MONEY

Yoga provides us with the greatest way to make and handle money, to give money its true value, and to use it to achieve success and happiness. I know how surprising this claim sounds. Indian spirituality is identified with renunciation and detachment from the world. Our typical image is of a white-bearded hermit, meditating in a cave high in the Himalayas. But, in reality, Yoga isn't spiritual in the religious sense. Yoga is the science of consciousness.

When you know how consciousness actually behaves, you find that something startling happens: You change with it. Learning about anything else doesn't have this dramatic effect. You might be enthusiastic, even delighted, to learn about anything else—history, geography, physics, etc.—but you won't be changed on the inside; you won't experience the personal transformation caused by Yoga.

There is an immediate connection to money, strange as this seems at first glance. At the soul level, there is generosity of spirit. This manifests as the following:

- *Infinite abundance*
- *Infinite possibilities*
- *Unlimited creativity*
- *Mercy, grace, and loving kindness*
- *Eternal love*
- *Boundless giving*

These gifts are innate and human awareness is designed to express them. If you embody them in your own life, you are wealthy in the truest sense of the word. Measuring wealth by money alone is spiritually empty. (I know nothing about reggae music, but the great reggae musician Bob Marley spoke like a yogi when he said, "Some people are so poor, all they have is money.")

To attain wealth of the lasting kind, the kind that gives your life meaning, value, and sustenance, base your daily existence on the generosity of spirit. Everything else you desire will follow of its own accord.

Once you make the connection between consciousness and money, you have stepped onto the right path. Money isn't all the gold in Fort Knox and all the dollar bills floating around in pockets and purses. Money is a tool of consciousness. Therefore, your state of awareness determines how you see money, how you gain it, and what you use it for. Consciousness is always in motion, and so is money. Consciousness motivates us to seek more out of life; money follows this journey and eases the way if you have enough of it.

If you shift your attitude away from money as the goal, but instead intend to get more out of life, you will have the support of consciousness. In Yoga this support comes from dharma, which comes from a Sanskrit verb that means "to uphold or support." If you are in your dharma, as it is usually phrased, abundance follows. If you are out of your dharma, you experience lack. Without the support of consciousness, nothing valuable can be achieved.

The concept behind money is powerful, and once it took hold (archaeologists trace the first money to the Mesopotamian shekel around five thousand years ago), money exploded as an idea. Behind modern life, the idea still flourishes. Seen as an invention of the mind, money accomplishes four different things that are necessary to human society. Money serves us as reward, value, need, and exchange. Pause and consider why you personally need money, and you'll see that all four things are present in your life.

Reward: The money slipped into a child's birthday card, the salary every worker is paid, and the tip left for the waiter in a restaurant are all rewards.

Value: The money slipped into the birthday card is pure giving, not needing to be earned. But it conveys that the child who gets the money is valued. The salary you earn expresses the value of your work, and for many people this becomes a way to measure their self-esteem.

Need: We live in a service economy that exists to fill people's needs much more than to provide physical necessities. When you need a doctor, a college education, a set of new tires, and a thousand other things, money brings you what you need, even seemingly superfluous needs, like this season's new fashion in sneakers or a bigger flat-screen TV.

Exchange: Money makes up the difference between two items that do not match in value. If you have a mountain bike for sale and I have only a dozen eggs to offer as barter, money has to be exchanged to make the bargain fair.

All of these ideas, and many more swirling around money, are the products of consciousness. This much it is easy to show. Yoga adds a missing ingredient, which turns out to be all-important. Yoga teaches that the closer you get to the source of awareness, the more power your consciousness has. By translating this power into things you desire, and the money to pay for them, you transform consciousness into wealth.

Money can't be sorted out from this tangle of good and bad choices. Because it is tied to everything we need, value, reward, and exchange, money is actually the coin of consciousness. You gain and spend joy, you experience love, friendship, family, work, opportunity, success, and setback, and money is always somewhere in the mix.

As Yoga sees it, consciousness is creative. It gives the mind thoughts, feelings, inspirations, breakthroughs, insights, "Aha!" moments, and everything else we value, including love, compassion, joy, and intelligence. The closer you are to the silent wellspring of consciousness inside you, the more you will receive these benefits. In the Judeo-Christian tradition, these benefits got translated into the fits of a merciful God, or Providence. But Yoga retained a focus on the self, not an outside divine power.

By keeping the focus on the self, we are not merely higher primates, but the expression of infinite pure consciousness. We exist to fulfill any creative possibility that we desire to pursue. There is no value judgment in Yoga. It is the science of consciousness, not a set of moral rules. Desires are all equal the instant they are born in our awareness. What kind of desire is good for us, however, is our personal responsibility.

DHARMA AND MONEY

The generosity of spirit is infinite. Therefore, nothing is more natural than abundance. What is unnatural is scarcity, lack, and poverty. I know that these are loaded words. All kinds of beliefs swirl around rich and poor, haves and have-nots. Social forces often work against the poor, and in no way am I casting blame or making a value judgment. Underlying all the inequality and unfairness, spirit isn't harmed or even affected. Take a snapshot of anyone's life anywhere in the world, and there is a path of dharma that spirit will support. It is always an inner path, and yet few people, East or West, rich or poor, understand how to gain access to their spiritual birthright. Yoga is the storehouse of the knowledge that is required before anyone can truly live the life they were meant to live, in fulfillment and abundance *from the inside*.

The key to wealth is being in your dharma, staying on the path that is best for you. "Best for you" is not defined in advance. You have a choice, and in fact you have been making choices your entire life that led to this moment in time. Look around, and the situation you find yourself in was mind-made. The physical appearances of a house, a job, possessions, salary, bank account, etc. are the results of consciousness. In and of themselves, material things have no intrinsic value. A mansion can be a place filled with unhappiness, a cottage can be filled with joy. A job can be a source of personal fulfillment or a grind. Your salary can bring you what you want out of life or barely keep your head above water.

If you want more out of life, construct a vision that dharma will support. In a moment I'll ask you to write down your personal vision of success, wealth, and fulfillment. But before that can be useful, you need to know which values dharma supports and which values it doesn't.

DHARMA WILL SUPPORT YOU IF ...

You aim to be happy and fulfilled.

You give of yourself to others.

You make other people's success as important as your own.

You act out of love.

You have ideals and live by them.

You are peaceful.

You inspire yourself and the people around you.

You are self-reliant.

You listen and learn.

You expand your options.

You take responsibility.

You are curious about new experiences.

You are open-minded.

You have self-acceptance and know your worth.

Because being in your dharma is the most natural way to live, these things are just as natural and easy to follow. But modern life doesn't guide us according to what is dharmic, and often quite the opposite. We are influenced to believe in a way of life that produces stress, distraction, unhappiness, and constant stimulation. These results come about when you live on the surface of your awareness. On the surface there is a constant play of demands and desires that have no deep roots. Their spiritual value is nil, meaning that there is no connection to dharma.

Yoga lays out the reality of how consciousness works. After that each of us can choose to live any way we want. You can get by knowing nothing about how your car works; it is just a useful, replaceable machine. But knowing too little about how dharma works causes many troubles. Unconsciously, we all work against the support of spirit in the following ways:

DHARMA CAN'T HELP YOU IF . . .

You are only out for number one.

You climb on the backs of others.

You do anything dishonest.

You blame others for your difficulties.

You are desperate to get rich.

You put material success ahead of happiness.

You ignore the needs of people around you.

You are certain that you are always right.

You seek to dominate and control others.

You ignore your stress level.

You are loveless.

You lack empathy and caring.

You take more than you give.

You are stubbornly close-minded.

Avoiding these things in general isn't difficult for most people most of the time. It's the small acts of selfishness, the casual disregard for others, a tendency to cast blame, and a habit of taking more than you give that can invisibly slip into your daily existence. Dharma isn't asking you to be a saint. It is asking you to be aware. When you are aware of all that spirit can give you, being in your dharma provides a source of joy.

The most valuable kind of awareness is self-awareness, because your dharma is guided not by superficial desires but by your true self, the self that is connected to your source in spirit. Over the years I've asked people to raise their self-awareness by answering a set of questions that go to the heart of their purpose for being here. Before we continue, I invite you to construct your own "soul profile," as I call it. Afterwards we'll talk about what it reveals.

READING YOUR SOUL PROFILE
How to listen to your true self

To achieve wealth while being in your dharma keeps you on the path that is right for you. This path is yours to define and shape. How? By consulting your deeper awareness, where inspiration and wisdom come from. We can call this deeper place your soul or true self. Messages from this level nurture experiences of happiness and fulfillment more surely than the mental activity that occupies the mind's surface. Keeping up a soul connection is how you remain in your dharma from day to day.

The beauty of the soul or true self is that it isn't on a time schedule. You can be preoccupied with life's demands and desires, and yet somehow messages come through from a deeper level. Each message silently reminds you of what is most valuable in life. All that is most valuable in human existence—love, compassion, creativity, wisdom, inner growth, insight, beauty, and truth—are already a part of you. This is true without exception. The light of pure awareness is eternal, and thankfully, at some level all of us are living in the light.

What you need to do is to match who you think you are with your true self. There is no need to strive for self-improvement. Your soul makes you valuable beyond measure. Right now, the main way that messages from the soul register is at the ego level. When you feel an impulse of love, beauty, empathy, insight, and all the rest that your soul imparts, a message has leaked through your ego defenses. The ego is nothing else but an imitation self, pretending to be the real thing.

TAKING THE QUESTIONNAIRE

With all of this as background, the following questionnaire will help you open up a connection with who you really are. In almost every case, this will be the same as who you dream you want to be.

INSTRUCTIONS

Find a quiet place, center yourself for a moment by taking a few deep breaths. Once you feel calm and centered, answer the following questions by tapping into your true self.

Suggestion: In order not to get swamped in long descriptions, keep your answers as short as you can. I generally recommend only three words—just be sure that they are three meaningful words.

1. Can you describe a peak experience in your life, something that was a major "Aha!" moment, a turning point, or a remarkable example of being "in the zone"?

   Answer: _____

2. In three or four words, what is your life purpose?

   Answer: _____

3. What is your proudest contribution to your family?

   Answer: _____

4. What are the three most important values you contribute to a relationship?

   Answer: _____

5. What are the three most important values you want to receive from a relationship?

   Answer: _____

6. Who are your three greatest heroes/heroines?

   Answer: _____

7. What are your unique gifts, skills, or talents?

   Answer: _____

8. How have you helped the world and the people around you?

   Answer: _____

9. What would you do if you had all the money and time in the world?

   Answer: _____

10. What is the most important thing you have wanted to accomplish but never did?

    Answer: _____

REFLECTING ON YOUR ANSWERS

The real purpose and value of these questions is to introduce you to your true self. If you are already living a life that brings fulfillment, you know your true self very well. There will be room for reaching higher and living up to your ideals even more than you have, but your answers won't reflect lost opportunities and faded dreams.

Most of us will find that we know our true self only in fits and starts. Unconscious behavior fills in the gaps much of the time, allowing us to identify with the self-image we project to the world. Happiness and fulfillment are more a fleeting inspiration than a daily reality. But at the level of our true self, we are connected to our dharma, which supports the life we are meant to be living. Despite the ups and downs we experience now, our dharma is there waiting for us to make contact.

It is valuable to save your answers and return to your soul profile on a regular basis. No one can give you an inner checkup but you. Answering these questions in a serious, reflective way puts you in touch with a deeper reality, and this expands your self-awareness. Your true self knows that you want to have a lasting connection with it, and if you focus on your soul profile, the connection can only deepen.

MONEY KARMA

Dharma works to support you in your intention to be wealthy and successful, first on the inside, then through the reflections that life gives back to you. Yoga teaches that the two worlds we occupy, in here and out there, are actually two aspects of one reality. A famous sutra, or axiom, of Yoga says, "As you are, so is the world." Outward reflections are the outcome of your intentions. Clearly, some people have much better reflections than others. If you want to have money, but your circumstances are far less than ideal, something has gone amiss. What you wanted and what you got are out of sync.

The culprit is karma, which lives in the gap between intention and outcome. Pause for a moment to consider your successes and setbacks up to now. Every life has both, even the most rich and glamorous (that's why we check in so avidly with celebrities, to dream about an ideal existence while reassuring ourselves that popular idols have troubles as bad as our own).

Karma is why bad things happen to good people. In modern secular society this sounds wrong. Bad things happen for all kinds of reasons, including random accidents, which have no reason at all. But the doctrine of karma covers the good as well as the bad. It is also the engine that does the opposite, bringing wealth and power to the undeserving. This makes the karmic setup sound very unfair. The rational mind wouldn't look at things this way at all. There is always the risk of blaming the innocent victim or overlooking the sins of the rich and powerful.

However, the doctrine of karma doesn't justify calling life fair or unfair. Karma is simply the leftover results of our past actions—in Sanskrit the word *Karma* simply means "action." An air of mystery surrounds the whole notion of good and bad karma, but in everyday life we totally depend on karma, because it is the same as cause and effect. If the connection between cause and effect didn't exist, nothing would be predictable. It would be a bizarre world if ice abruptly caught on fire or if chocolate unexpectedly tasted like fish.

Whenever people refer to good karma and bad karma, what they generally have in mind is good or bad luck. Out of the blue, somebody wins a fortune from the lottery or, at the other extreme, loses everything they have when the economy crashes. At a higher level of complexity, karma implies something more: Where luck feels accidental, karma is woven into the complex scheme of cause and effect. Once you cause something to happen, the effect is inevitable. It seems as if karma, keeping track of all your actions—good and bad—follows you around, keeping you trapped in situations you want to escape, sometimes desperately.

Does such a thing exist, an invisible force that overrules our best intentions or brings sudden rewards almost with no effort? This was never the purpose behind the theory of karma, which doesn't imply a fateful force beyond our control. Action is certainly under our control, and the only thing that the doctrine of karma adds is unforeseen consequences, which is not an alien or exotic concept.

If you look at every action you have ever taken, along with the consequence of each action, the sum total is your personal karma. Can this calculation actually be made? No, not in the course of everyday life, because there are simply too many actions entangled with too many consequences to remotely calculate. (In Hinduism there is also the factor of actions performed in a prior lifetime, but we won't be tackling reincarnation, which for our purposes is irrelevant—the actions you perform in your present lifetime give you a great enough challenge.)

Karma only becomes practical in daily life if you reduce it to factors you can change. As applied to your present circumstances, your karma comes down to the following:

- Habits

- Automatic reactions and reflexes

- Unconscious behavior

- Character traits

- Predispositions, including gifts and talents

As you can see, there is a host of behavior patterns we can call "karmic," not because they are innately harmful but because they have no obvious cause. Karma cannot assign a cause for Mozart's genius or the attention deficits of a young child struggling in school, or even why some people are always cheerful and others always gloomy. Neither can modern psychology offer reliable answers. Innate dispositions, like musical talent, aren't genetic—a musical genius like Leonard Bernstein didn't even come from a musical family, and he famously defied his father Sam, who wanted him to sell hair products.

Geniuses of every kind have been born into completely ordinary families. The same holds true, as every mother knows, with infant behavior. The intimate bond between mother and baby puts her in a position to see personality and character emerge from day one, and telltale signs appear that will come to fruition as the child grows up.

If karma doesn't offer explanations, how can it be useful? Its primary use is to give you the choice to live unconsciously or consciously. Think of the first karmic category—habits. No one has to be told how hard it is to break a bad habit, and sometimes a whole society adopts one, as in the current epidemic of obesity. Almost everything associated with overeating—lack of portion control; snacking; eating fatty, sugary fast food; and a sedentary lifestyle—develops unconsciously. It's in the nature of habits to creep up on us unwittingly until we, or someone else, notices them, and by then the habit is likely to be deeply ingrained.

Studies have repeatedly shown that a slim percentage of dieters, somewhere around 2 percent, manage to lose as little as five pounds and keep it off for two years (the other 98 percent don't lose any weight or else lose weight only to gain it back). This lamentable statistic testifies to the power of unconscious behavior. No karmic mystery is involved, yet that doesn't reduce the power of a karmic force we generate on our own, through years of unconscious habit.

Knowing that you overeat or seeing that you look fatter in the mirror isn't the same as being conscious of a solution. You are merely becoming aware at the level of the problem. Karma is overcome by going to the level of the solution and finding clarity. In the case of overeating, people try all kinds of solutions that do not break the habit, largely because karmic patterns are constant, while the desire to eat less comes and goes, subject to how a person feels at any given moment.

If you examine the problem more closely, it is useless to continue to fight a war with yourself. This leads to vacillation, self-recrimination, and little or no progress toward a solution, no matter how much you swear to yourself that you will take advantage of your gym membership. Overeating is generally solved by one or two methods. Either the person wakes up one day, says "Enough is enough," and carries through by suddenly finding that the temptation to overeat is gone. The other possibility, which is far more common, is that a person, reducing the problem to one of calories, decides to rigorously count every bite of food eaten in a day, recording the calories in a notebook to prevent cheating and unconscious lapses.

I've used the example of a common habit to illustrate something crucial: *Karma only changes if you find a way to be more conscious.* Struggling against any kind of karma amounts to struggling with yourself. If the warring impulses inside you could come to a truce, they would have done so a long time ago. You know this from the impulses that you have already brought into balance. Take any serious personal problem—phobias, worry, runaway anger, envy, self-doubt, shyness, depression, an abusive relationship, unloving parents—and some people will find their lives drastically hindered by the problem while others have dealt with it and moved on.

Karma isn't inexorable. If you are stuck, the remedy for getting unstuck is always at hand through self-awareness. The most common money problems that can be called karmic are listed below.

QUIZ

What Is Your Money Karma?

Answer each of the following items on a scale from 1 to 10, where

1 = Not a problem

5 = Occasionally a problem

10 = A serious problem

___ You have a hard time balancing your monthly checkbook.

___ You have credit card debt.

___ You are saddled with long-standing bank or student loans.

____ Your mortgage is too high for your income.

____ You are not seriously planning for retirement.

____ You splurge on luxuries, usually on impulse.

____ You have caviar tastes without the income to match.

____ You argue over money with your spouse or partner.

____ You worry about your financial future.

____ You can't see a way out of your present financial difficulties.

____ You are living from month to month on your salary, just making ends meet.

____ You foresee expenses you cannot afford, such as paying for a child's education or putting an elderly family member into assisted living.

____ You have never been able to save money.

____ Learning about finances and investing is beyond you, or you don't care enough to try.

____ You have fallen behind on your taxes.

____ You don't take financial advice when it is offered.

____ You consider money a forbidden subject.

____ You spend on things you later regret.

____ You disapprove of how your partner or spouse spends money.

____ You resent your low salary from work.

Total score _____

ASSESSING YOUR SCORE

If you are perfect with money, giving yourself a 1 on all 20 items, you probably don't exist. Being perfect is as remotely likely as having the worst possible score of giving yourself a 10 on all 20 items.

Most people will find themselves around an average of 5 × 20 items = 100. In other words, your finances are habitually a worry if you examine them with clarity. Some things are working out well, while others are not. The point isn't really a numerical total but those items, or issues, that you rate as 7 to 10. You can look on these as danger points, in which case you will only add to your worry and continue as before.

On the other hand, each item you classify as a worry contains a choice, and the choice is almost always one of expanded awareness. Only what you are aware of is open to change. There is nothing to fear from being more aware. You are already aware of your problems at the level of the problem. The shift you need to make is to become aware of them at the level of the solution.

Ultimately, you need to regard the use of money simply as a compensation. People treat money as the route to happiness when the actual route, bliss-consciousness (which we will discuss in more detail in Part Three of this book), is closed to them. Being self-aware isn't the same as a promise to get rich. But self-awareness helps to put money in proper perspective, as useful but nothing to obsess over if you want a fulfilling life. Many money issues will melt away of their own accord once you come to that realization.

MONEY KARMA CAN IMPROVE

Every problem has a level of solution in your awareness. Being more aware gives you the basis for change. In terms of changing your money karma, the following things are self-defeating because they are unconsciously driven by old habits and past conditioning:

- Worry, anxiety

- Inertia

- Denial

- Wishful thinking

- Giving up

- Hiding from yourself

- Pessimism

- Self-judgment

We all are subject to these futile tactics, and the more sensitive the issue, the more likely we are to resort to them. Money, of course, is a very sensitive issue. It is tied to a sense of personal failure or success. Having money rates you a success in society's eyes; not having money makes you invisible and overlooked. However, most people have very little knowledge about how to approach their money karma in a positive way.

Here are the tactics that bring a change in karmic patterns because they are linked to self-awareness:

- Clear perception

- Honesty with yourself

- Seeking expert help

- Persistence

- Believing that a solution exists

- Trusting that you will find the solution

- Realistic thinking

- Being open-minded about your choices

- Taking responsibility

- Doing what you know you need to do

If you consider the two lists, you will see that in other aspects of your life outside of money you act quite consciously. There are no karmic hang-ups, so to speak, when you do anything that brings you joy or arouses reactions of love, beauty, sympathy, appreciation, and a sense of being fulfilled. Money isn't something that brings forth these experiences in and of itself. Money can either help you to have such experiences or block your way. Your strategy toward your money karma should revolve around that realization.

IMPROVING YOUR MONEY KARMA

1. When you find yourself doing anything on the list of what doesn't work, stop doing it. This is the most important step.
2. Don't struggle against the impulse of worry, self-judgment, wishful thinking, denial, etc. Instead take some downtime quietly by yourself until you feel calm and centered.

3. Whenever you are feeling generally good about things and have time to reflect, look over the list of positive choices. Select a change that you can realistically make, asking yourself one of the following questions to reflect upon:

- How can I get clear about something that's a challenge?
- Is there something I have to be honest about?
- Where can I look for good advice?
- What's one good thing I really need to persist with?
- Do I believe a solution is possible?
- Do I trust that I can reach the solution?
- Am I being realistic about where I stand and what my situation is?
- Can I be more open to new choices?
- How can I take more personal responsibility?

4. Once you have chosen a question, let it sink in. These are not formulaic questions but lines of communication with your true self. Just sit quietly with the question. Don't struggle or strain to find an answer.

5. Now wait for a response. Whether immediately or very soon, a deep level of awareness will bring you a response. It might feel like a message or an "Aha!" moment or simply a new direction opening up.

6. Once you feel that an answer has come, act on it. Whatever action you take should be in line with your

own comfort and your values. Money karma won't improve through worry, obsession, self-blame, or panic-driven choices. What you are learning to rely on is a deeper awareness.

7. Your true self is always on your side, and learning to be aligned with it brings you to the level of solutions and away from the level of the problem—nothing is more important. We'll be discussing how to connect to your true self as this book unfolds.

THE DOUBLE BIND

There is one tangle between money and karma that needs mentioning. Personal karma consists of repetitive patterns that you can change. Expanding your awareness will expand your choices. Expanded choices bring fresh opportunities, and new opportunities allow solutions to unfold. This is the gist of a money strategy based on how consciousness really works.

But there is a karmic block I'd like to bring up that is collective and social, meaning that you were born into it, along with everyone else. Money has created the ultimate illusion. Trapped in this illusion, money is what you crave but also fear. Wealth is impossible to achieve when you are stuck following your fear. A psychologist would call this kind of inner contradiction a double bind: You desire and fear the same thing simultaneously. You cannot free yourself from the illusions surrounding money until you escape this double bind.

Shakespeare hit upon a primary teaching of Yoga in the final couplet of Sonnet 64. The poem is one of gloomy resignation. It begins by noticing a commonplace occurrence, that riches and power, no matter how great, are transient. The ocean constantly wears away the shore. The highest towers are worn down to rubble. The sonnet escapes the commonplace by turning psychological at the end:

> *Time will come and take my love away.*
> *This thought is as a death, which cannot choose*
> *But weep to have that which it fears to lose.*

The double bind has never been expressed so succinctly. Desire makes us chase after everything we love, and yet once we have won it, there is automatically the fear of loss. Is the double bind universal? Shakespeare thought so, and Yoga agrees. The difference is that we can look upon the double bind as a complete illusion, which is the key to finding a way out.

The path is quite clear. Don't crave money and don't fear it. Put your time, thought, and energy into reality, which is the flow of creative intelligence. The clarity of this teaching is almost blindingly obvious. Who doesn't prefer reality to illusion? Unfortunately, the answer is "all of us." To be fixated on money is an offshoot of being fixated on materialism. The one follows from the other. Basing your life on getting more material things, however, is enough to close off the path of consciousness.

In Buddhism, the path of consciousness includes right thought, right speed, right action, and right living. Yoga includes these things in its teaching about dharma. Dharma isn't materialistic. Success depends on being aligned with the same human values Buddhism espouses. Without them, accumulating money would deserve its reputation for being not spiritual, even the opposite of spiritual. I hope this conception has been dispelled for you. What lies ahead is a vision of abundance that encompasses every aspect of life—mind, body, and spirit.

MONEY AND WORK

If you work for a living, you probably like your job—according to one prominent survey, job satisfaction is not only high, it took a leap recently from 81 percent in 2013 to 88 percent in 2016, the most recent year for such data. Such a high percentage can't help but be surprising. It seems to imply that people in general must be thriving, but this is far from true. Fewer than a third of people describe themselves as thriving, which leaves two-thirds struggling or just getting by.

How can there be such a gap? The answer is adaptability. Workers adapt themselves to fit the jobs they do. From the perspective of "follow your bliss," work should be about who you are. Yet in most people's lives the opposite is true. Who they are doesn't matter very much. What matters is holding down a job, doing it well, and hoping for a raise. To turn this around and make your work about you, we need to start with the basics.

First, the most satisfying jobs aren't necessarily the highest-paying. Doctors in this country are highly paid, on average, and if you train to become a surgeon, you have good prospects for becoming rich. But out of the fifteen most satisfying jobs, physicians rank number eleven and surgeons are near the bottom at number fourteen, just above teachers. The number one position would shock almost everyone: The most satisfying job is to be a member of the clergy. One very high-paid job, being the

CEO of a company, turns out to be very satisfying (number two), but you can be almost as happy at work if you are a chiropractor (number three) or a firefighter (number six). The police are not anywhere on the list.

What actually counts isn't so much your job or your job title as the conditions under which you work. This has been measured through studies in social psychology. If you want to know why you love or hate your job, consider the following factors.

SATISFYING WORK CONDITIONS

Job satisfaction rises if your workplace gives you certain key things:

☐ Money (but only up to a certain point)

☐ Low stress

☐ Job security

☐ Good relationships with coworkers

☐ A sense of being heard

☐ Loyalty and support from higher-ups

☐ The chance to care for others

☐ Opportunities for advancement

☐ Positive company culture

☐ Challenging daily tasks

☐ Being good at your job

If you measure your job by this list, the more boxes you can check off, the happier you will be at work. That's true as far as it goes. But lists and charts don't really represent human nature.

Most people can work around a horrible boss one way or another. Countless workers do jobs that are so routine and mindless that there is no chance for day-to-day challenges, so they compensate by finding an offsetting positive, such as forming a strong friendship at work. Two supermarket cashiers chatting all day will discover more happiness than a doctor swamped by his patient load and mountains of paperwork to fill out.

Aligning yourself with creative intelligence comes down to practicalities in the workplace. The whole point of creative intelligence is that it aims for the best outcome for yourself and those around you. This isn't magical thinking. In everyone there is a level of consciousness that seeks solutions to problems, and when you operate from this level, you are aligned with the flow of creative intelligence. When you do the opposite and focus on problems with an attitude of complaint, worry, and blame, you are stuck at the level of the problem instead.

Now that you know the most important elements that lead to job satisfaction, you can turn your attention to improving them at your own job. Using your energies this way is better than complaining, stewing with resentment, or passively putting up with the status quo. Taking active steps is always self-empowering. If you find yourself in such an environment, move on to another job as soon as you can.

Money

You should be making what you think you are worth. That, rather than getting more and more money, is a psychologically healthy goal. Unfair wages cause more dissatisfaction at work than almost anything else. A company culture that doesn't pay fair wages doesn't respect their workers, either.

Money is tricky, and you might be fairly paid without improving your situation. This generally happens because someone is deep in debt (mainly through credit card debt) and so overextended financially that money is a source of constant worry. Look at your situation and take responsibility for the portion of money worry you have caused yourself.

The best way to take responsibility is at the level of awareness: Stop asking money to do things it cannot do.

- More money won't make a bad job bearable.

- More money doesn't make you better than people who earn less.

- More money won't give you self-esteem.

- More money won't make others like you more, although they might do a good job pretending to.

Changing these attitudes, if you see them in yourself, means that you are taking personal responsibility by putting your true self ahead of your salary, however high it is.

Low stress

Most job stress comes from well-documented sources: the pressure of deadlines, too heavy a work burden, multitasking, excessive noise, and job insecurity. At the same time, stress tends to get into the atmosphere and become contagious. If you actively want to reduce stress, you need to take two steps: Fix the stressors that are affecting you and don't cause stress in others at work.

The ideal is a quiet, congenial atmosphere where everyone is focused on one task at a time without undue pressure. Is that too much to ask? Only you can be the judge, since no two workplaces are exactly alike. A nearly silent accountant's office bears little relationship to a noisy construction site. The ultimate judge is the bodymind, which is the holistic system that unites both body and mind as one. If you are having a hard time getting enough sleep, worry about deadlines, need a drink after work, bottle up resentments, easily get irritated and impatient, lose your appetite, or generally feel fatigued and stretched too thin, these are the most basic early warning signs that you are under too much stress and need to do what you can to remedy the situation.

As for not putting stress on others, the formula is simple: Think about the things that make you feel stressed, and, once you are aware of them, don't do these things to your coworkers or those working under you. The keyword is pressure. Be aware of feeling too much pressure and do something about it, rather than passing the pressure along.

Job security

Next to worrying about not having enough money, people feel the greatest anxiety about job security. Even in Japan, once famous for corporations that hired workers for life, the typical corporate practice everywhere has deteriorated. Pension funds have been stripped, and workers' rights have declined, largely because of fear over not having a job. As individuals, you and I have no power over business practices, but in the last two major economic downturns, the 2008 Great Recession and the massive job loss caused by the COVID-19 pandemic, it became evident that it was small businesses that cared for the welfare of their workers, shared the burden, and attempted to come up with equitable ways to keep their employees working.

Your role is to assess the company you work for and your current situation with clarity and sound reasoning. Are employees cared for, and in what ways? Does the welfare of the workforce really matter to management? Do your coworkers feel secure? Ask and find out. Then consider how much weight you place on job security. In some jobs, like restaurants, job fluidity is natural, while in others, like the civil service, knowing that you will probably always have a job is a major attraction.

Be realistic about your present situation, but also look to the future. America is a country with few social safety nets, high consumer debt, a high rate of eating out, low rates of savings, and little protection offered by organized labor. With these factors in place, along with the fact that until COVID-19 took so many lives, more and more people were living longer, it is only realistic to assume at an early age, decades before retirement, that you will have to provide for yourself financially between ten and thirty years if you retire at sixty-five. The picture is quite sobering when you consider the amount of savings that financial experts, including government calculations, recommend by age group:

- Americans in their thirties: one to two times annual salary recommended

  versus

  Actual median savings: $21,000 to $48,000

- Americans in their forties: three to four times annual salary recommended

  versus

  Actual median savings: $63,000 to $148,000

- Americans in their fifties: six to seven times annual salary recommended

  versus

  Actual median savings: $117,000 to $223,000

- Americans in their sixties: eight to ten times annual salary recommended

  versus

  Actual median savings: $172,000 to $206,000

As a rule of thumb, you should start saving 10–15 percent of your annual income starting in your twenties and look forward to living after retirement on 80 percent of your annual income right now, according to standard financial advice.

No matter where you fall—many people are doing better and many are doing worse than average—it is your lifelong responsibility to make yourself secure in the future. Pollsters find that the greatest fear among the elderly isn't ill health or death but becoming a burden to their children. More and more, this fear is coming true for millions of Americans, thanks to low savings, inadequate pension plans, high living costs, and the exorbitant expense of care for patients with Alzheimer's (or even the healthy elderly). To avoid being part of the negative statistics, the answer is the same as for every aspect of money: You can only change what you are aware of. Without awareness, you are prey to circumstances outside your control.

Good relationships with coworkers

This point might seem self-explanatory, because getting along with your coworkers is more desirable than the reverse. In reality, however, there are glitches. Some people at work are impossible to get along with because of their difficult personalities. Other people are selfish and have no regard for anyone else, or they might be so competitive that they cannot be trusted. Office gossip spoils relationships, as do office romances. In short, the workplace is as complex as human nature itself.

Your role is not to be one of the negative types just mentioned. Friendly cooperation should be your norm. You will also improve your relationships with coworkers by doing the following:

- Listening when someone else is talking.

- Not showing favoritism or choosing sides.

- Showing vocal appreciation when a coworker does something well.

- Lending a hand when you see that a coworker is under stress or pressure.

- Always showing respect.

- Refraining from gossip and office politics.

- Being sympathetic to another person's version of events, even if you disagree with it.

- Realizing that everyone has a story and believing in their story.

This may seem like a long list, but, at bottom, every item results from being aware, rather than unaware. Once you are aware of how group psychology works, meaning the group you find yourself in, you can behave as your awareness dictates. Few people are actually flexible enough in their psychology to alter relationships when difficulties appear, so the best advice is to foresee the difficulties and avoid them in advance.

A sense of being heard

Studies of job satisfaction put being heard higher than most of us would because there's always an imbalance in the ego's agenda: What I have to say is more important than what others have to say. Even when this factor isn't dominating, it is easy to forget that every person you encounter wants to be heard at least as much as you want to be heard.

If you find yourself working in an environment where the higher-ups don't listen to you, that is a major warning sign that you are in the wrong job. When managers refuse to listen, your contribution is basically that of a drone, and you can expect your feelings of frustration, resentment, and helplessness only to rise.

Loyalty and support from higher-ups

Every kind of work, with very few exceptions, is arranged as a hierarchy. There will be someone above you (unless you own the company or are a CEO), which limits your independence and freedom simply because things are set up that way. To feel comfortable anywhere in a hierarchy, you need to trust those above you. That's the trade-off for giving them power over you.

Many people passively accept a situation where the trade-off is completely out of balance. They are expected to be loyal while those above them are untrustworthy, whimsical, arbitrary, closed off, or otherwise wielding power unfairly. If you have anyone under you at work, your role is to avoid those pitfalls. Looking at those over you, take seriously the silent bargain that exists between workers and bosses. If the bargain is a bad one, consider whether you are in the right job. Bringing unfairness to a bad boss or manager's attention rarely improves the situation and often leads to retribution.

The chance to care for others

The clergy, nurses, and physical therapists stand high in job satisfaction because of a common denominator: They have the opportunity to care for others. Such caring is based on empathy and the desire to help. The opposite situation exists among caregivers for Alzheimer's patients, where the burden is constant, the end hopeless, and the response from the person being cared for is negligible or worse. It is a considerable challenge to our society that being a caregiver for patients with dementia shortens the caregiver's life expectancy on average by five to eight years, a direct result of high daily stress.

The vast majority of jobs are not in a caring profession, but you can show sympathy and care in any line of work. Take the opportunity to show someone else that you care, even if it's only by a warm smile or a passing remark. Don't follow a formula or ritual. Be personal and sincere. Modern life increases the possibility of feeling isolated and lonely, particularly among the poor and the elderly. Keep this reality in mind, because your well-being depends on how much support you have from friends, family, coworkers, and support groups. If you give support, you are much more likely to receive it in the future when you find yourself in need.

Opportunities for advancement

Years ago, I met a media mogul who was unusual for arousing very little envy, animosity, fear, or resentment around him. If one of the mega-rich can be loved by the people who worked for him, it was this man. His secret was simple. He aimed to make every associate as rich as he was. To him, this was the secret of his success, because he earned so much loyalty when his employees understood that he was eager and willing to give them every opportunity for advancement.

I imagine that such behavior is rare today. Some major corporations, particularly in Silicon Valley, have created corporate cultures that benefit their workers with all kinds of comforts at work. At the individual level, the urge to put yourself first suits the ego's agenda. But if everyone wants to get ahead, acting as separate selfish entities is one of the worst ways to raise your actual chances for getting ahead.

Your role is to find a job where there is opportunity for advancement—still no easy thing for women. This part can be challenging, which accounts for why there is so much fluidity in the American job market. The trend, however, is not moving in your favor. Upward mobility has declined in the United States, and other nations, such as the Scandinavian countries, now offer more opportunities. Upward mobility is also skewed toward educated white males. If you have only a high school degree, your opportunities have been declining for decades. A Black man with the same education as a white man will likely have only 50 percent of advancement at work.

Looking realistically at these odds, many people have resigned themselves to remaining in a relatively static job that is likely to offer few advancement opportunities. You must decide how your situation stands and what your expectations are. Also keep in mind the media mogul I mentioned. Creating opportunities for others is a winning strategy. One for all and all for one is a viable way to get ahead. Find the people whom you see as allies, and make alliances, connections, and networks as a regular part of your career arc.

Positive company culture

Company cultures are moving up from a very low, even disgraceful, starting point. Heroes of American capitalism emerged from a brutal tradition of exploiting workers. When Henry Ford built his model of a car assembly-line plant at River Rouge outside Detroit in 1928, he created a work environment that was inhumanely noisy, stressful, mindlessly boring, and low-paid. Yet one reads much more about the success of the Model T and Model A Ford than about the horrendous corporate culture those cars came out of.

Jobs that come with benefits are at a premium today, and 99 percent of workers can only look with envy on the 1 percent who work for companies like Google and Apple that provide humane, comfortable working conditions. But even these companies are entangled with Chinese factories that would be outlawed as sweatshops in America.

Individuals cannot influence company culture unless they are very highly placed in the hierarchy. Your role is to put your well-being before money. Work where you feel good mentally and physically. At a minimum, you deserve this level of working conditions. If problems exist, consider working from home or changing jobs. Settling for an ugly company culture is motivated by fear and insecurity. Motivate yourself by your level of well-being instead—that's what this book is all about.

Challenging daily tasks

One viable reason that job satisfaction has risen so much is the decline in boring routine work. Painful as the transition is, retooling factories so that robots do the bulk of routine work is moving society in the right direction. Already 37 percent of American jobs can be done from home, which is a more congenial setting than an office.

But raising the floor isn't the same as aiming for the sky. Human consciousness thrives on challenge if the challenge is creative. In a nutshell, this should be your personal aim. Money, responsibility, status, power, and prestige are weak compensations by comparison. The drive to succeed makes people settle for promotion over creativity, and that is a bad trade-off.

What is a creative challenge? It can be defined as any possibility that allows you to expand your gifts and talents. These are the possibilities that make you feel that you are growing and evolving, getting better at what you are already good at, or expanding into a new field that excites you. It isn't necessary to be a creative artist. Wherever solutions and innovations are valued, creative challenges abound.

Unfortunately, society doesn't teach us about the real perils of boredom and burnout. Becoming a physician holds high social value, but doctoring has a very high rate of drug abuse and burnout. There are few creative challenges when your day is filled with anxious patients who will wind up being treated the same way with the same procedures and medications. (I speak from experience in my early, driven, pre-burnout years as an endocrinologist in Boston; my eventual salvation was to find a creative way to be in the healing profession, a path I had almost no models for among the young doctors I knew. They were as trapped as I was but in more denial about it.)

Do something new every day, and you will be renewed. That's not a fantasy. Every cell in our body exists through constant renewal. Do you deserve as much as a liver or a stomach cell? The question is very much worth asking.

Being good at your job

Wanting to be good at their jobs comes naturally to almost everyone. Doing a good job earns respect and admiration. People will treat you better than if you do a sloppy or careless job. But it is easy to go too far. If you identify with your job, the rest of your life will shrink. People who are all about their work have become a common type. Working long hours, taking work home, striving for perfection—these are symptoms of a troubling condition. Ambition is not a virtue.

You can approach this issue in terms of hours during the day. Time scheduling is working for our well-being if you have room for the following:

- Moving and stretching for five minutes every hour.

- Finding time to connect personally with someone you feel close to (not via texting or email),

- Making time for yourself, alone and quiet.

- Doing something that feels like play or recreation.

- Spending quality time going inward, meditating, or doing yoga.

If your day doesn't contain these elements, or if you look upon them as occasional luxuries, you aren't using your time to advance your well-being. Of course, time scheduling isn't everything, much less be-all and end-all. Relationships have a value that transcends any daily schedule, but there is still the practicality that you can't have a rewarding relationship unless you make enough time for it.

So, when you consider what it means to be good at your job, look closely at how each day unfolds. If you are squeezed for time, preoccupied with work every hour, and saddled with too many duties and demands to meet without stress, you are the victim of time. From the viewpoint of creative intelligence, there is always enough time to do what is best for you. Align yourself with that truth, and you will be on the path to making every day fulfilling and not just the part of your day where you are working.

THE FLOW
OF CREATIVE INTELLIGENCE

Being in your dharma opens a clear path for the dynamic aspect of consciousness, which has been dubbed "creative intelligence." Yoga teaches that pure consciousness isn't static. It vibrates with life and is driven from within itself to emerge into physical creation: i.e., the universe. The flow of creative intelligence organizes all living things on Earth, but alone among all life-forms, humans can consciously tap into creative intelligence, which we have done for millennia.

When you emerged from the birth canal, you brought with you no memory of your life in the womb, no memory of your journey from a single fertilized cell into a newborn baby. In the same way, how we attained the ability to create is lost to human memory. Let me give possibly the most ancient example of hominin creativity, a single creative act that made civilization possible. Every animal runs away from a fire when it breaks out in the wild through a lightning strike. Why did *Homo erectus* turn around and, instead of running, imagine that fire could be tamed? What magical transformation turned fear into ingenuity?

Anthropology offers no answers. It was long held that fire had to be the product of *Homo sapiens*'s greatest evolutionary attainment, a huge higher brain. Of all species, the human brain is by far the largest in comparison to body size. Then traces of wood ash began to appear in sites once inhabited by *Homo erectus*, who had a much smaller brain. Instead of the previous estimate that fire came under control perhaps 100,000 years ago, which predates the most ancient cave paintings by 70,000 years, archaeologists began to find ash in sites one million years old, which predates *Homo sapiens* between 800,000 and 970,000 years, depending on which estimates you accept. This date of one million years has wide acceptance, but on the fringes are reports of ash deposits that are much older, even up to two million years old.

Our hominid ancestors didn't need a modern cerebral cortex of immense size to tame and use fire; they needed only awareness, which was open to creative intelligence. That is the perspective of Yoga, which teaches that consciousness is self-aware, self-organizing, and self-sufficient. Creative intelligence, entirely of its own accord, inches us toward the next new discovery. Whatever creative intelligence is able to do, which is infinite, we are able to do. The chain can never be broken.

The electricity that powers the modern world is an update of that first impulse to tame fire, just as your smartphone and desktop computer are updates of a mental skill developed in the late Stone Age: counting. The most ancient artifacts from the Neolithic era are stones scratched with holes in a row—indentations made, it is supposed, to trade goods between tribes. Holes in a row only make sense as stand-ins for numerals. There are no numbers in Nature; numbers are a creative construct invented by humans.

MONEY AS EVOLUTION

All your life you have been embedded in the flow of consciousness. You think, feel, speak, and do. Each of these activities requires a conscious mind. When Yoga was formulated at least a thousand years ago in India, and probably much earlier, the ancient seers had no raw material to work with, no psychology departments, research studies, textbooks, or professional experts—only what arose in their own minds. It is miraculous that these explorers of the world "in here" made discoveries worthy of Einstein. Even today Western psychology has miles to go before catching up.

A major discovery was that consciousness wants to evolve. Being creative, it flows toward curiosity and discovery. Fueling this impulse is a feeling of joy whenever we make a new discovery—young children can't conceal their delight at finding out some new wonder in the world. Besides being joyful, the things we discover add value and meaning to our lives—just ask anyone in the first flush of romantic love, a discovery that for a time exceeds any other when you are infatuated and walking on air.

Love can come out of nowhere like a blinding flash, but most of the time we have a choice. We can choose to evolve, we can choose the opposite, to go backwards. Here's a simple diagram that physics applies to the universe and everything in it:

CREATION

←—————— *ENTROPY EVOLUTION* ——————→

Throughout creation since the big bang, two invisible forces have pulled in opposite directions. The first, evolution, creates complex forms, starting with the swirling, chaotic energy immediately after the big bang, which led, over billions of years, to atoms, molecules, stars, galaxies, and planet Earth. But tugging in the other direction is entropy, which breaks down these structures, leading to physical decay, dissolution, and a steady loss of energy.

Yoga teaches that human consciousness is pulled in opposite directions by the same forces—order and chaos. The evolution of consciousness has dominated the history of *Homo sapiens*. Despite the entropic effects of war, disease, natural disasters, and psychosis, which sap evolution and drag existence downward, the flow of creative intelligence constantly drives evolution. This includes money, because for five thousand years money and commerce have made civilization possible—progress always comes with a price tag.

Inside us, entropy can be thought of as whatever saps our own creative intelligence—unconscious behavior, habits, conditioning, inertia, close-mindedness, and passive inertia. We need only one more diagram to fill in the human condition, meaning the place where you and I find ourselves in the theater of life:

THE HUMAN CONDITION

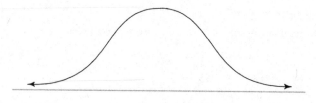

— ENTROPY *(habit, inertia, unconscious behavior, etc.)*

versus

CREATIVE INTELLIGENCE ⟶

All of us live under the bell-shaped curve. The vast majority of people are clustered in the middle. Here there is a mixture of entropy and evolution or, as the popular saying has it, "two steps forward, one step back." Because most people lead lives filled with unconscious choices, habits, conditioning, prejudices, fears, hopes, and dreams, their unconscious impulses are strong and lead to entropy: i.e., wasted time, money, emotional investment, and emotions. There will also be evolution mixed in, because in the conscious part of our lives we create, love, feel inspired, and find joy.

Yoga teaches that it is possible to increase the ratio of conscious choices and, when this happens, you move away from the middle of the curve toward accelerated evolution. At the thinnest edge on the right, where evolution is most advanced, we find the motley crew of geniuses, saints, sages, artists, and visionaries. They exist, as it were, on the tip of the tree, reaching upward with nothing to guide them but pure consciousness. Without aspiring to join them, each of us can choose to evolve. This isn't Darwinian evolution, which is physical, but the evolution of consciousness.

Since money was born in consciousness, it can go in either direction, too, toward waste and loss or toward gain and creativity. To be very practical, since money is very practical, here's what entropic choices look like, the kind that wind up not getting you anywhere you want to go:

ENTROPY: HOW WE GET MONEY WRONG
Seven things that don't work

1. Fantasizing about money

For many people, money is a dream and getting rich a beautiful fantasy. This doesn't work because reality isn't the same as fantasy. No one who is actually rich calls it a dream come true, and yet we harbor the fantasy anyway.

2. Money as an end in itself

Without a doubt, having money opens the way for improving your life. But when making money is an obsession, it starts to substitute for actual fulfillment. Anyone, rich or poor, who wakes up every day wanting to make money is going to create a wider gap between money and happiness.

3. Fear of poverty

Want and lack are a source of misery, and no one who has suffered from being poor wants to return to that state. But if your motivation is fear, then poverty still has you in its grip. Anxiety is never correlated with growing happier.

4. Cheating, dishonesty, lying

Society holds up images of wrongdoers who got rich by scheming, and unless they get caught and are sent to jail, schemers are usually proud of themselves. They have beaten the system. They are no suckers, like everyone who plays the game honestly. But, in reality, only the slimmest percentage of people lack a conscience. Dishonesty generates guilt, and, like anxiety, guilt is the enemy of happiness.

5. Betraying your core beliefs

Short of lying and cheating, many people feel that they have been forced into dull, routine, and unfulfilling work. They feel that circumstances pressured them into this situation, but at bottom they are engaging in self-betrayal. The two most important core values are "I deserve to be happy" and "I have strong self-esteem." Unless you uphold these values, you are moving in the wrong direction.

6. Abusing other people

Stepping over other people to get ahead is hardly ever considered the right thing to do, but we do it anyway. The whole ethos about looking out for number one is powerful. So, we overlook those occasions when we put other people down, ignore their feelings, seek to dominate them, and adopt selfishness as an excuse for misbehaving. Abusing others to get your own way actually indicates that deep down you feel inadequate.

7. The "killer instinct"

If winning is everything, then the ultimate winners are hypercompetitive. They have the killer instinct for taking advantage of weakness, and the smell of blood in the water excites them. But, in reality, few of us can thrive in a shark tank, and we wouldn't want to. Anyone fixated on being a winner at all costs is secretly driven by a deep fear of being seen as a loser. No amount of success makes this fear go away.

When you line up all the things people get wrong, it is no wonder that evolving proves so difficult in everyday life. We are entangled in a value system that traps us into lives that fall far short of fulfillment. The process of getting entangled happens over time, and we give in to mistaken beliefs almost unconsciously. Do you know breadwinners stuck in jobs they hate? Is losing your job a fear you find hard to face? Have you ever met someone who was once well off but then went broke?

Those experiences, which all of us have had, act on us, consciously or unconsciously, at some time in our lives. The worst aspect of going in the wrong direction is that you feel helpless. But you have more choices than you realize. You can untangle yourself by adopting choices than work. Money can be made while increasing your sense of happiness and well-being.

CREATIVE INTELLIGENCE: HOW WE GET MONEY RIGHT
Seven things that actually work

1. Self-sufficiency

Financial independence is worth seeking, and most people hope to get there by the time they retire. But far more important is feeling independent inside. True self-sufficiency means following your core values, not giving in to other people's opinion about you, and knowing without a doubt that you are enough.

2. Taking responsibility

When you blame other people and outside forces, you are giving away your personal power. Taking responsibility for your own life is empowering. It puts you in contact with the things that need changing inside yourself, and therefore you open the way for change to actually happen. Giving up your responsibility keeps you stuck as a victim.

3. Cooperation

Cooperation bucks the ethos of winner-take-all and looking out for number one. Despite the fantasy of being the big winner, life isn't a zero-sum game. Unlike the Super Bowl, which decides the sole winner and loser, cooperation creates a constant stream of win-win outcomes. Aiming for such an outcome also produces a sense of fulfillment when you make money for others as well as yourself.

4. Work ethic

Society isn't mistaken when it advises that a sound work ethic is important. But what actually works is a *good* work ethic or, as Buddhist teaching would affirm, "right work." Hard work by itself is rarely right work if it involves struggle, toil, and the postponement of happiness until your retirement years. Working at what you love brings fulfillment here and now. Then no amount of hard work feels like work at all.

5. Being true to yourself

Feeling blissful is the hallmark of your true self, and the surest way to know that you are not betraying your core values. Being true to yourself should be a joy. If you identify with your ego instead, you are basing everything on an insecure foundation. "I" is a false guide because it never runs out of desires, excuses, fears, envy, and blame. Identify instead with experiences that bring secure fulfillment.

6. Be faithful to your core values

Values has become a loaded political word for stubbornly held beliefs and bald-faced prejudice. Core values are different. They involve love, compassion, truth, loyalty, self-esteem, humility, and personal growth.

Keep in mind that the highest values in life mean nothing until they are *your* highest values.

7. Focus on awareness

You cannot change anything in your life unless you are aware of it first. Awareness isn't the same as logic and reason. You can't figure out consciousness; it is a given, the source of everything in creation. Your role is to align yourself with the flow of consciousness, which means doing your best to make evolutionary choices with your time, effort, emotions, and money—they are important.

Outlining what works and what doesn't work is useful because it is practical. Most people stick with behavior that doesn't work out of habit. They usually don't even know why. We indulge in self-defeating behavior over and over again merely out of inertia.

The best way to live is on the path of evolution; therefore, the best way to earn and use money is on the same path. There's a more metaphysical issue at hand, however. The hidden mystery in creative intelligence is this: Are we using it or is it using us? This question makes sense when you look at childhood development. Moving from early infancy onward, a child makes momentous discoveries, such as walking, that involve no conscious choices. No infant arrived at the toddling stage by thinking, "Hmmm, all those bigger people are moving upright on two legs. I should give it a try." Crawling on all fours works for every other animal. Even in the primate world, an ape or monkey, despite being able to walk upright for a short time, doesn't keep at it. They always prefer using arms as if they were legs.

You and I weren't allowed a preference. We learned to walk through an inner impulse that worked inside us. It was an impulse of creative intelligence using us for its own purpose. You can see in a toddler's face the mix of wonder, fear, and delight as walking begins to dawn. A gift is being given, and the child finds it irresistible to take the gift, yet there's a good deal of uncertainty surrounding the process. Reverting to crawling feels safe; falling flat on your face feels painful. But a toddler risks pain in the moment for a skill that will prove enormously useful in the future. A toddler has no conception of the future, but creative intelligence does. In fact, it knows a lot about the future, and thank goodness for that; every step toward language, advanced motor skills, and higher thought unfolded in you because an inner impulse was already in place to guide you.

Creative intelligence is consciousness in action, and once you connect with it, you are on the way to untold rewards. When Einstein declared that no great discovery in science can be made without a sense of wonder, he connected the highest achievements of the mind with the gleam in a toddler's eye on discovering how wonderful it is to walk. There are new worlds to discover when wonder expands to meet them.

SIMPLE AWARENESS

What you are aware of, you can change. That part isn't complicated. Obviously, you can't change what you are not aware of. Awareness, however, is actually the most powerful engine for change, which isn't widely known. Here we need to broaden our perspective. Your attitude toward money, as we saw, is entangled with everything else you want and fear, dream about and aim to achieve. For a moment, let's look at the bigger picture. Yoga teaches that the more you know about consciousness, the more clearly you can see the path to success and wealth.

Dharma is constantly showing the way forward. Inevitably, the way forward involves change; therefore, dharma signals where the next change should occur. Anytime you have a moment of sudden insight, the change comes instantly. Again, there is no mystery involved. If you suddenly remember that you were supposed to meet someone at three o'clock, you rush out the door because your realization is all it takes to motivate you.

There are deeper insights that come more rarely, but I can recall people who personally told me that the following realizations changed their lives:

- I am an adult.

- I really belong.

- I am loved.

- I am lovable.

- I'm good at what I do.

- I'm a good person.

- I'm a genuine person.

- I matter.

The words are simple, but their impact for these people was life-changing, because it wasn't the words that held such power but a shift in awareness. Such insights are messages from the soul, or true self. Because they tell us something true and indelible about ourselves, the change they bring is an "Aha" that makes life feel different from that point on. You can do good works all your life to prove that you are a good person, yet on the inside you are actually trying to convince yourself more than others. An insight that tells you, without a doubt, that you are a good person requires no struggle and brings no doubts. Then the good works you do come naturally and bring you joy.

To bring about sudden change isn't something you can plan, control, or schedule. The soul has its own way of timing the experiences we call epiphanies. But you can cultivate the state of awareness that opens the way for insight and revelation. This state is known as simple awareness, and reaching it is effortless.

Simple awareness is the silence between two thoughts, the gap between the ending of one thought and the beginning of another. In everyday life this gap flashes by so quickly that we don't notice it, but in simple awareness the gap between thoughts lasts longer than usual. Instead of a new thought popping instantly into your head, you experience quiet mind. This is more than a quick reset for your brain. You are having an experience that has its own flavor, its own signature. If I break this down, you will certainly recognize what I mean.

How Simple Awareness Feels

- Quiet, calm, peaceful

- Contented

- Relaxed

- Complete

- Open

- Undisturbed by thoughts

- Without memory

- Without need, desire, or fear

Simple awareness is baseline. It is not a goal you must seek and run after. You can glimpse it after finishing a great dinner or when appreciating a great work of art, while listening to Bach or listening to your child at play. These glimpses are proof of an important teaching in Yoga: The mind naturally seeks its source. It will connect to your soul, or true self, if given an opening. Your mind doesn't have to be coaxed to go there, much less forced.

The mind is thrown out of simple awareness all the time. You might assume that what throws it out is the next thought, but that's not it. The gap between two thoughts changes. It can be shallow or deep. When you are anxious, panicky, excited, agitated, or restless, thoughts start to race, and the gap between them feels anxious, panicky, excited, agitated, or restless. For the time being, as long as you feel this way, your baseline isn't deep, calm, and relaxed.

There is a helpful yogic image for this, known as drawing back the bow. In archery, you draw the bowstring back, and, depending on how far you can draw it, the arrow shoots forward with more velocity and power. The mind works the same way. In between two thoughts you draw your mind back in silence, and from there you launch the next thought. We refer to "deep thinkers" for this reason, recognizing that when they pause for thought, they are going more deeply in their awareness than the ordinary person. But it isn't the thought that is deep; it is the arrow let fly from deep awareness.

With meditation, you can make your inner silence deeper still, because, as noted above, the mind naturally wants to find its source; it wants to be connected to the soul. What we need is a way to get back to simple awareness, as illustrated in the following chart.

HOW TO REACH SIMPLE AWARENESS

Simple awareness is here and now. You are either in it or you are somewhere else. Your mind has been pulled away to a state of awareness that overshadows simply being here now. This can happen through daydreaming or a temporary distraction. More serious are the times when you are pulled into a negative feeling. If you find yourself feeling the same negative emotion persistently—for example, frustration, anger, anxiety, or depression—you are not aware of the present. Instead the past is coming back for an unwanted visit.

Here are three specific situations that arise in our lives and ways to return to simple awareness.

1. REPETITION AND BOREDOM

When you feel bored and the "same old, same old" discourages you, you are not in simple awareness. Unwittingly you are not present. The present moment is creative, because it opens the way for new thoughts, feelings, and inspiration. Your mind naturally wants to be in the now unless it gets distracted. If you find yourself feeling distracted, stressed, or disengaged, the best thing to do is to center yourself.

The practice is quite simple. Find a place where you can be alone, close your eyes, and take a few deep breaths.

Now center your attention on the heart region in the center of your chest. Breathe in deeply by filling your belly region so that it pushes outward. Now slowly exhale. At the end of the exhale, pause for a count of 1, 2, 3, and repeat.

This simple method of controlled breathing is known in Yoga as *Pranayama* and in Western medicine as vagal breathing (named after the vagus nerve, which is crucial for the relaxation response). The technique is one of the most useful, quick ways to become centered and relaxed, and enter into simple awareness.

2. NEGATIVE BELIEFS

Simple awareness is open, but it is common to find that your mind is loaded with automatic reactions. People get stuck on ingrained beliefs that are discouraging, self-defeating, judgmental, and generally negative. For example, you might find yourself believing the following:

- Life is unfair.
- The world is a threatening place.

- To get along, you have to go along.
- No one will look out for number one but me.
- You have to claw your way to the top.
- Nothing good happens to the little guy.
- Life sucks, and then you die.

These beliefs get stuck in our minds without knowing where they came from or why we believe them. Since beliefs are formed in the past, they throw you out of the present. Your awareness is neither simple nor open and clear.

There are similar beliefs that crop up in challenging situations like going out on a first date or going to a job interview. You start to believe self-defeating thoughts because they are emotionally gripping, making it hard for you to see things rationally and clearly. Typical examples:

- This isn't going to turn out well.
- Something's bound to go wrong.
- I've been here before, and I smell trouble.
- I can't cope with this.
- It's all too overwhelming.
- Why did I ever think this would work out?

These immediate reactions are born of habit. They reflect a belief that you are not adequate to meeting the situation. If such thoughts are blocking your vision, first try centering, as described above.

If you still find it hard to get back to a calm, centered state, you need to perform some self-care. This doesn't happen on the spot. You must find a time when you are quiet and calm inside, and then do a little investigation into the roots of the problem. Take any negative or self-defeating belief, and you will see that it has lodged in your mind because of the following specious conditions that confront all of us:

- We believe the first person who told us something.
- We believe things that are repeated often.
- We believe the people we trust.
- We didn't hear a contrary belief.

When you find yourself stuck on a negative self-belief, something that makes you feel bad about yourself, pose the following questions:

- Who first told me this?
- Was it repeated a lot?
- Why did I trust the person who told me this?
- Is there reason to believe the opposite?

In other words, you need to reverse the experience that made you latch on to a belief in the first place. By turning the past around, you gain insight into how your mind got stuck.

If your mother told you that you aren't pretty or your father that you are lazy, why should you automatically trust them? It doesn't matter how often you heard their opinion. Now that you are an adult, you can separate opinion from fact. Go back and consider experiences that indicated how attractive you are in other people's eyes or how diligently you applied yourself to a task that truly interests you. This reversal of old imprints, in itself, is healing, and you can be in simple awareness again.

3. BAD MEMORIES

Perhaps the most common way of being stuck in the past occurs in memory. Old wounds and traumas return, warning us not to repeat something bad that happened in the past. The stickiest part of a memory is its emotional charge, which some psychologists have termed "emotional debt," something that everyone has. We stubbornly hold on to old resentments, grievances, fears, and wounded feelings like old debts that haven't been paid off and cleared.

This gives us a clue to getting unstuck. Instead of trying to remember the time nobody came to your birthday party, notice the feeling this bad memory brings up. Instead of revisiting a relationship that ended in recriminations, focus on the feeling you get from the memory. Memories are hard or impossible to erase, but emotional debt can be discharged.

The following techniques for discharging emotional debt are easy and effective. Emotions, by their very nature, rise and fall, and most of the time a cooling-off period suffices to return you to a settled state. But sticky (i.e., stubborn) emotional states don't fade away on their own. They ask you to assist by discharging them through various practices.

TECHNIQUE #1: If you feel an uncomfortable emotion that persists, center yourself and take slow, deep breaths until you feel the emotional charge start to lessen.

TECHNIQUE #2: If you recognize an emotion that has been around a long time, notice its return, then say: "This is how it once was. I am not in the same place now." Awareness defuses the intensity of negative emotions, but this intensity varies from person to person. The key is not to push such feelings away. If you sit with a negative emotion with the intention of embracing it in your awareness, this technique can be very effective. Thanking an emotion for coming to your attention and then sitting quietly until it fades away is much better than resisting it. Resistance only makes the unwanted emotion try even harder to get your attention.

TECHNIQUE #3: With a particularly stubborn emotion, sit quietly with your eyes closed and let yourself feel the emotion—do this lightly, not sinking deeply into it. Take a deep breath and exhale slowly, releasing the emotional energy from your body. It might help to see your breath as a white light, carrying the toxic feeling out of you.

TECHNIQUE #4: If you feel no specific emotion, but rather a general mood of being down, blue, or out of sorts, sit quietly with your attention placed in the region of your heart. Visualize a small white light there, and let it expand. Observe the white light as it expands to fill your whole chest. Now expand it up into your throat, then your head, and up out the crown of your head.

Take a few minutes to carry this technique through until it feels complete. Now return to your heart and expand the white light again until it fills your chest. Now see it expand downward, filling your abdomen, extending down to your legs, and finally out through the soles of your feet into the earth.

These four techniques can be applied separately or one after the other. But it is important to be patient. Once you use a technique, it will take time for your whole emotional system to adapt to the discharge. In short, everyone suffers from some kind of stuckness, but now you are in a position to be aware of what is happening and to take steps to return to simple awareness. Simple awareness lets you live in the now, where reality is renewed and refreshed.

PART TWO

FINDING YOUR ABUNDANCE

Yoga applies to money in ways that hardly anyone expects. But looking even more deeply, Yoga approaches life as consciousness on the move. Thanks to the generosity of spirit, consciousness doesn't move around randomly, like playing darts while blindfolded. The dharma benefits and supports us. Far beyond money, dharma is always on your side. We can simplify this with one word: *abundance*. If you have enough money, you are rich. If you have abundance, you are fulfilled. This is the true aim of Yoga.

Psychological studies show that having enough money makes people feel better, but, beyond a certain point, adding more money actually lowers a person's sense of happiness. There's a crucial question each of us asks at one time or another: "Is this all there is?" These five words suggest feelings of lack and unfulfilled dreams. We are confused about why other people have more than we do—more love, greater financial security, more confidence, and greater success. Money is only a small aspect. You might be unfulfilled in your career or relationships. At the worst of times, you might experience more suffering than joy. Worst of all is a sense of emptiness. In our darkest moments, these feelings leave us anxious, resentful, and lost for answers.

People use all kinds of tactics to get around their lack of fulfillment. These tactics include fantasy, wishful thinking, endless consumerism, constant distractions, and denial. Being materially well off doesn't solve the problem. In its global project of measuring people's sense of well-being, the Gallup Organization uses two indicators—surviving and thriving. *Surviving* means that you are just getting by; *thriving* means that your life is going well. There is no objective standard for the two; people are simply asked to pick one according to how they feel. Even in the richest, most developed countries, only about a third of respondents tell Gallup that they are thriving. The "have-nots" outnumber the "haves" by a huge factor if you glance around the world.

THE ATTITUDE OF ABUNDANCE

If I've painted the picture right—and I think most people will recognize themselves in it—there is an urgent need for abundance. Yoga equates fulfillment with an attitude of abundance. This is close to what Gallup is measuring. Either you have an attitude of abundance (thriving) or an attitude of lack (surviving).

Two-thirds of people in prosperous societies have an attitude of lack, which is emotional and psychological. It has nothing to do with the size of your bank account. Without confronting our attitude of lack, you and I have silently fashioned our sense of self around limitation. We are careful about what we wish for. We fear going beyond our safe boundaries and secure comfort zones. These habits have actually shaped our identity. I knew a man who squandered a windfall of over a million dollars. He was intelligent and sensible, and he had always managed his personal finances well. After the money was gone, he had an insight. "I see myself as a $40,000-a-year person," he told me. "A million dollars wasn't who I am. So I managed to get back to $40,000 a year despite everything."

An attitude of abundance changes your expectations, your behavior, and even your identity. Without fulfillment, there is no point in adding more money and consumer goods to your life. H. L. Hunt, a fabulously wealthy oil billionaire from Texas, was famous for wearing old shoes with holes in the soles and a cheap suit from JCPenney's—these were remnants of an impoverished early life in barren East Texas. He never acquired the attitude of abundance, which is where our story really begins.

QUIZ

Where Are You Now?

If you set out today to make your life more abundant, your starting point would be different from anyone else's. People in your income bracket, or above and below you, have inner attitudes and beliefs about abundance. These shape the outcome their efforts will yield even before they start.

Directions: For each of the following statements, check *Agree, Neutral,* or *Disagree.* Trust your first response. If you feel fairly weak on the Agree or Disagree side, it is better to choose one than to check Neutral. Doubts and second thoughts tend to cloud the issue, rather than clarifying it.

PART 1: ATTITUDE OF LACK

The people who get rich are usually greedy.

Agree ☐ Neutral ☐ Disagree ☐

Money is the root of all evil.

Agree ☐ Neutral ☐ Disagree ☐

When someone gains, someone else has to lose.

Agree ☐ Neutral ☐ Disagree ☐

I tend to notice my inadequacies.

Agree ☐ Neutral ☐ Disagree ☐

I am blocked in reaching my goals because I remember my past failures.

Agree ☐ Neutral ☐ Disagree ☐

It is spiritual to take a vow of poverty.

Agree ☐ Neutral ☐ Disagree ☐

The people around me should support me more.

Agree ☐ Neutral ☐ Disagree ☐

Things go wrong if you set your expectations too high.

Agree ☐ Neutral ☐ Disagree ☐

In my heart of hearts, I don't feel like a success.

Agree ☐ Neutral ☐ Disagree ☐

I have no idea why some people fail and others succeed.

Agree ☐ Neutral ☐ Disagree ☐

You don't get anywhere unless you earn it.

Agree ☐ Neutral ☐ Disagree ☐

Bad people play the game better than good people.

Agree ☐ Neutral ☐ Disagree ☐

The important thing is to hold on to what you have.

Agree ☐ Neutral ☐ Disagree ☐

PART 2: ATTITUDE OF ABUNDANCE

If I set myself a goal, I am confident I will reach it.

Agree ☐ Neutral ☐ Disagree ☐

It's true that you can make your own luck.

Agree ☐　Neutral ☐　Disagree ☐

Opportunity is there if you look for it.

Agree ☐　Neutral ☐　Disagree ☐

I believe in being generous with my time, money, and resources.

Agree ☐　Neutral ☐　Disagree ☐

An attitude of giving has served me well.

Agree ☐　Neutral ☐　Disagree ☐

I can forget my past failures fairly easily, compared with most people.

Agree ☐　Neutral ☐　Disagree ☐

People are basically good.

Agree ☐　Neutral ☐　Disagree ☐

Everything happens for a reason.

Agree ☐　Neutral ☐　Disagree ☐

My life has a strong purpose.

Agree ☐　Neutral ☐　Disagree ☐

My work is meaningful to me.

Agree ☐　Neutral ☐　Disagree ☐

ASSESSING YOUR ANSWERS

This isn't a quiz with a numerical score, but you can still get a good idea of your starting point with abundance. It would be rare, if not impossible, to agree with all questions on both parts of the quiz, since they ask about opposite attitudes. Instead, you will find that you checked Agree and Disagree in varying proportions.

You have an **attitude of lack** if you Agree with six or more statements in Part 1. (You probably also marked Disagree on a number of statements in Part 2.) This is indicative of any number of things, such as

- Self-doubt
- Low self-esteem
- Skepticism
- Pessimism
- Memory of past failures
- Received opinions
- Defensiveness
- Financial insecurity

These factors are about you and your belief system, not about the world "out there." You are more likely to take self-defeating actions and make impulsive decisions. It's probably hard for you to set higher goals without feeling a sense of defeat before you take the first step. I am not assigning blame. Sadly, the world unfairly throws up obstacles to achieving success and abundance. You can't change the world, but you can change the inner obstacles you have put up.

You have an **attitude of abundance** if you Agree with six or more statements in Part 2. (You probably also marked Disagree on a number of statements in Part 1.) This is indicative of any number of things, such as

- Self-confidence
- Optimism

- Self-reliance
- Moving on after setbacks
- A strong support system
- Acceptance of others
- A nonjudgmental attitude

These things give you inner strength and resilience in the face of obstacles. You are not self-defeating when you take action and make key decisions. You are more likely than most people to be emotionally stable and to see situations with clarity. Setting higher goals doesn't make you anxious or raise specters of defeat.

You are probably *in denial* if you marked Neutral more than five times on either part, or if you marked Agree more than five times on both parts. The statements you were quizzed on are potent, and it is unrealistic to feel neutral about many of them. Denial is a safe position to take, but it is also a limiting one. Venture little and little is gained. This goes for our desires, wishes, and dreams as much as for the risks we take.

If you want an attitude of abundance, begin with simple awareness. As we saw earlier (page 49), simple awareness is a state of calm, quiet mind that feels centered and untroubled. In itself, simple awareness achieves only the first half of fulfillment, which is a sense of not lacking. The second half is arrived at by how your life unfolds. You want to feel fulfilled at work, in relationships, in your family life, and in your spiritual aspirations.

This is where consciousness comes in. Being in simple awareness, you start to witness changes that prove, to you personally, that dharma is supporting you. The generosity of spirit would be merely a nice idea unless your life actually changed. Human beings are complex and no two people have the same expectations. Even so, there are a great many ways in which fulfillment comes to us.

HOW FULFILLMENT UNFOLDS

- You begin to live in the here and now, ignoring the voice in your head that repeats a litany of old fears, wounds, setbacks, and disappointments.

- You banish worry as pointless and unnecessary.

- You act generously, instead of selfishly.

- You stop relying on someone else's approval.

- You stop fearing someone else's disapproval.

- You claim responsibility for your own emotions and reactions.

- You renounce blame.

- You let your creative impulses emerge.

- You respond from your heart.

- You look for beauty, love, and joy while you stop looking for flaws, problems, and worst-case scenarios.

- You practice appreciation, attention, and acceptance.

- You embrace your inner sense of self.

- You create your own bliss.

- You offer sympathy to those who need it.

- You are of service wherever you can be.

- You stop resisting and start joining the flow.

As you can see, the attitude of abundance has to be more than mere optimism or positive thinking; it goes deeper than a belief system or a matter of faith. Abundance must become part of your identity, as expressed in the phrase "I am enough." When this is your truth, then the world is enough at the same time.

Because human beings are complex, fulfillment has many aspects. The Japanese have a concept known as *Ikigai*, which is defined as "a reason for being." If you can attain Ikigai, whose roots can be traced back to traditional Japanese medicine, your life will be fulfilled. To get there, a person must take action aimed at four main goals:

- Love

- Things you are good at

- An affordable lifestyle

- What the world needs

Abundance has no value if these four areas are not fulfilled. You can't count up love the way you can count up jars of peanut butter, frozen pizzas, and cars, yet we all know the difference between emptiness and fullness in matters of love. Ikigai opens our eyes to how a life of purpose and meaning is constructed. The concept, which is part of daily life for millions of Japanese, originated on the island of Okinawa at an unspecified date in the past, although the word *Ikigai* itself can be traced to as early as the eighth century CE.

One virtue of Ikigai that doesn't appeal to Western society is that it puts everyone on the same page, keeping the common good foremost in mind. Individuality is secondary. This is considered important by a people as conformist as the Japanese. But there is no novelty in ascribing happiness to the purpose-driven life; or rooting your purpose in something you passionately believe in—both concepts are centuries-old.

Another variant is found in India, where, to this day, children are taught that the four aims of life, as laid down in the most ancient spiritual traditions, are Artha, Kama, Dharma, and Moksha.

- *Artha* is prosperity in material terms.

- *Kama* is fulfillment of love, pleasure, and desires in general.

- *Dharma* is morality, finding a righteous way to live.*

- *Moksha* is spiritual fulfillment through liberation or inner freedom.

The words in Sanskrit shouldn't mislead us into thinking that these are merely Indian concepts. The reason that a child born in any generation, including me, was taught these four values is that they have universal appeal. By implication, all four goals are attainable by anyone. Moreover, life will become distorted unless you pay attention to each goal. Look around, and you will witness the imbalance that results when only Artha, or material prosperity, and Kama, the pursuit of desire and pleasure, dominate to the exclusion of the moral and spiritual side of life. They add meaning to abundance, and the one thing human beings cannot tolerate for long isn't poverty, but a meaningless life.

---

* Sanskrit words have a range of meanings, and *dharma* is casually used to mean your way of earning a living.

Let's accept that the two models of an abundant life from India and Japan are desirable; almost no one would disagree. But are they achievable? Here is where aiming only at material abundance starts to come apart at the seams. When we say "Money can't buy happiness," the problem isn't money but the word *buy*. Happiness isn't transactional. You can't put a price on it because the whole commercial scheme of pricing, buying, exchanging goods for services, getting the most bang for your buck—none of this makes sense when what you are after is inner affluence. Life becomes fulfilling only when you act from the level of meaning.

However, countless people approach a new relationship with commercial intentions, even if they don't realize it. From a transactional viewpoint, going on a date involves a checklist of desirable qualities, like the checklist you'd apply to buying a new car. The relationship is based on ticking off boxes to make sure the prospective lover is attractive, prosperous, smart, funny, not too self-centered, and willing to pay attention to you. Yet none of these boxes, even if all of them are checked, says that a relationship will actually be meaningful. A rich, fulfilling relationship, like a rich, fulfilling life, comes from the inside.

PUT FULFILLMENT FIRST

Yoga embodies a great truth: Everything we could ever possibly need is available in generous supply. An attitude of lack runs contrary to this and therefore falsifies the reality. Among all living things, human beings have been given the whole package that Nature has to offer. Our species can eat almost any food, adapt to and live on any part of the globe, speak different languages, choose from endless thoughts, and pursue equally endless desires.

Every type of abundance "out there" grew from a seed idea "in here." Each of us lives in the flow of creative intelligence that turns invisible desires and dreams into physical reality. There can be no doubt that the whole package is your birthright. Unfortunately, many of us don't realize the inner power we have to create a beautiful world. And, as you'll see, *not* living with the whole package has seriously impacted your life. This deficiency cries out for healing and transformation.

Seeing only limited possibilities creates hardship and suffering, but can an attitude of abundance in and of itself get you where you want to be? Clearly not. There is real life to contend with—traffic, weather, global health issues, economic highs and lows—and, for the vast majority of people, daily existence looks like this:

_____ Ideals _____

"Real Life"

_____ Expectations _____

The diagram is simple but alarming. We can see visually that a gap exists between the ideals we cherish and what the world "out there" actually allows us to have. "Real life" deserves to be in quotation marks because everyone has a different conception of what real life actually is. Obviously, it is not the same to be born poor instead of rich, a girl instead of a boy, a person of color instead of white. Yet whoever you are, you are likely to believe that real life was the cause, perhaps not the only cause, but the major one.

To demonstrate what I mean, below is a list of common beliefs we've all been exposed to (a few have already been mentioned earlier). Many people tend to accept these beliefs, in varying degrees, without much thought. Take a moment to see which ones you casually believe in, or perhaps more than casually.

COMMON BELIEFS ABOUT "REAL LIFE"

- Life is unfair.

- It's all a roll of the dice.

- You have to go along to get along.

- Look out for number one—nobody else will do it for you.

- The world doesn't owe you a living.

- Easy come, easy go.

- You can't fight city hall.

- A sucker is born every minute.

- You're either a born winner or a born loser.

- Life sucks, and then you die.

The above list could be titled "Ten Easy Ways to Lower Your Expectations." I must emphatically state that these beliefs contribute to the attitude of lack. Even knowing this, however, it can be hard to break free from their influence. One antidote is to shine a light on these beliefs to expose the false lessons that we've taken as truth. Let's look at these common beliefs a little more closely.

Life is unfair.

False lesson: *By its very nature, reality is set up to defeat happiness.*

It's all a roll of the dice.

False lesson: *Random chance is in charge. It defeats good people and rewards bad people all the time.*

You have to go along to get along.

False lesson: *Conformity is the only safe way to live.*

Look out for number one—nobody else will do it for you.

False lesson: *Selfishness should be your first concern.*

The world doesn't owe you a living.

False lesson: *Nothing good happens without toil and struggle.*

Easy come, easy go.

False lesson: *Getting what you want doesn't last.*

You can't fight city hall.

False lesson: *Power always beats out justice.*

A sucker is born every minute.

False lesson: *Most people exist to be taken advantage of.*

You're either a born winner or a born loser.

False lesson: *Destiny is out of our hands.*

Life sucks, and then you die.

False lesson: *The world is a vale of tears, ending with nothing to show for it except extinction.*

We are all in the habit of believing that "real life" is set up to get in the way of what we want for ourselves. When misfortune arrives on a mass scale—through war, natural disasters, the economy going bust, or a totally unexpected shock like a global pandemic—these events serve to reinforce our belief that real life has the first and last word. As our expectations get hammered, our ideals steadily become pie in the sky, wishful thinking, and a huge disappointment.

What can we do except play the game and take our chances? Yoga teaches that "real life" must be confronted in a new way. There has to be conscious expansion of the possibilities we are willing to accept; otherwise, self-imposed limitation will never go away on its own. To create this expansion, Yoga relies on two things: attention and intention.

The *law of attention* holds that whatever you put your attention on grows.

The *law of intention* says that the world "out there" obeys your deepest desires.

When you put these two laws together, the result is known in Sanskrit as *Sankalpa*. The common definitions of *Sankalpa* are a heartfelt desire, a vow, or a resolution to act. The best understanding, however, is "subtle intention." At its subtlest, a Sankalpa needs no words. If you intend to lift your arm, the intention is enough. If you start to speak, your intention draws together a remarkable number of elements: the action of your lungs, vocal cords, tongue, etc. Besides these body parts, your intention to speak brings forth words, and the words depend on activating your memory, vocabulary, and the ability to string everything together to make sense.

There's no doubt that subtle intention is astonishing, except that we take it for granted. Put under the microscope, however, the power of intention reveals itself by what gets silently accomplished.

- A desire moves from the invisible to the visible world.

- Your intention is automatically linked to its fulfillment.

- Every ingredient seamlessly meshes.

- Self-organization guides the whole process.

A medical science researcher can spend a lifetime understanding the mechanics of speech, with input from pulmonologists to neurologists and everyone in between. Let a single step go awry, and it can lead to disaster. But in everyday life, we simply let Sankalpa take care of everything, and, in thousands of ways, it does. Intention brings us everything we have ever gained from life.

The sticking point is that moving your arm or starting to speak happens "in here," inside the bodymind. If you want the world "out there" to obey your wishes, any competent psychiatrist would look worried. "Magical thinking," as it is known, is a symptom of delusion, psychosis, or a very overactive imagination—except in Yoga.

Yoga recognizes no separation between "in here" and "out there." Your intentions have a level playing field. You can intend to lift your arm or to meet the person who will turn out to be the love of your life. Both intentions can be organized through Sankalpa. Therefore, it achieves exactly what we've been looking for, a way to turn an attitude of abundance into actual abundance.

The flow of creative intelligence is universal—it functions everywhere. You can steer the flow through your intentions, in other words, your desire. The rules are clear-cut in yogic terms.

THE PROCESS OF SANKALPA

- Be in simple awareness.
- When you feel calm and quiet inside, form an intention; that is, an outcome you'd like to see.
- State the intention once, then sit silently for a few minutes.
- Let go of the intention, assuming that you will get a response.
- Be on the lookout for a response with an open mind.

Every time you think, speak, or act, these steps occur, since it takes an intention before anything happens in the bodymind. There is no reason to believe that carrying out a Sankalpa outside your body is any different. Society doesn't teach us that what we want makes any difference in the outside world, however. Everyone who buys a lottery ticket, plays a competitive sport, or wants anything else that other people also want, knows what it is like to be disappointed. When there is a zero-sum game, there can be only one winner.

How does Yoga deal with this? By looking a little more deeply into how dharma works. We get the support of dharma under the right conditions and lose the support of dharma under the wrong conditions.

RIGHT CONDITIONS

- You have a clear intention.
- You feel no confusion or conflicts inside.
- You want what is good for you; i.e., what is most evolutionary.
- You want to do no harm to others.
- You want the best outcome for everyone.
- You are in your dharma.

Some of these conditions make perfect sense, but others seem unattainable. How can you know what is evolutionary for you? How can you predict which outcome is best for everyone? A skeptic might call the whole thing sleight of hand—you are promised to have your dreams come true, but then the promise is withdrawn, putting the blame on you.

But this ignores the power of Sankalpa because if your desire meets the right conditions, you will have your dreams come true. When you are aligned with the flow of creative intelligence, outer obstacles vanish. Disappointments and setbacks occur because the wrong conditions were present.

WRONG CONDITIONS

- You have mixed intentions.
- Your intention was simply a whim or a passing desire.
- You are not in simple awareness.
- What you want will harm others.
- What you want is too far outside your dharma.
- You interfere with the process, instead of letting it unfold automatically.

The magic of Sankalpa is that it works automatically. You don't have to investigate or interfere, just as lifting your arm doesn't require you to know anatomy or to winch your arm up to help your muscles along. The popular adage "Everything happens for a reason" takes the right attitude, which is one of optimistic trust. Have your intention, let it go, and see what happens.

Two things are the major obstacles to Sankalpa: inattention and karma. Inattention means that you forgot to keep watch for a response. Intentions come true, almost all the time, by a sequence of steps. If you want to meet your true love, sitting in front of the TV waiting for the doorbell to ring won't work. You have to pay attention to see what to do next. Your true self knows what to do next. It has already connected your Sankalpa with the right outcome. After you make your intention clear, there will always be a signal about what comes next. It might be an inner signal, perhaps a casual desire to meet a friend of a friend who was suggested to you. But more likely you will continue to do what you typically do, except that at some level you will know that Sankalpa is working its invisible gears.

The second obstacle, karma, is the wild card. Set patterns from the past may block the outcome you want. I don't mean that karma is inevitable. As we saw earlier (page 12), money karma can be improved. The steps recommended there work in general. The key thing is that karma is never a total obstacle; it only diverts your expectations. A good example is running a marathon. Only one runner will break the tape at the finish line to be declared the winner. But the other runners can experience the satisfaction of completing the course, improving their best previous time, or proving something to themselves. A sense of fulfillment makes every Sankalpa worthwhile.

Nothing you really value in your present life—a loving relationship, a good family, worthwhile and rewarding work, and the time to enjoy these things—came about by chance. They grew out of desire and intention. If you get nearer to your true self, the power of intention grows stronger. At your source in pure awareness, this power expands without limit. The actual experience is one of increasing bliss. The blissful life is open to everyone, and "follow your bliss" has deep roots in Yoga, as we are about to see.

PART THREE

THE GIFTS
OF CREATIVE
INTELLIGENCE

THE CHAKRA SYSTEM

If you want to maximize the abundance in your life, you need to use your awareness better and better every day. In other words, you need to evolve. There is an evolutionary flow to human awareness, which is embodied in creative intelligence. Yoga is quite specific about this. There are seven qualities of creative intelligence that have the highest evolutionary value. Think of these as the gifts of creative intelligence because they are just that.

SEVEN GIFTS OF CREATIVE INTELLIGENCE

- Bliss

- Intelligence

- Creative expression

- Love

- Successful action, self-empowerment

- Sensual pleasure, sexuality

- Security, safety

There is abundance in every gift. The generosity of spirit could not be more visible. If you evolve in these seven areas, you will live out a vision of abundance unknown to most people. No one needs to be persuaded to think that these gifts represent something valuable. Who wouldn't want to feel blissful, rather than miserable? The advantages of making smarter choices and more effective action are self-evident. Unfortunately, life isn't organized around these gifts for all kinds of reasons. The first of these reasons is our inability to navigate inside our own minds.

Every day, each of us is immersed in a constant stream of thoughts, sensations, desires, feelings, hopes, and worries. For most people, the stream of consciousness is too much. They are not helped by being told that they have infinite potential, which is fundamental in Yoga's teachings. As promises go, this one is overwhelming. If you saw infinite possibilities in your life, you would be paralyzed, the way some writers are paralyzed looking at a blank piece of paper. Assuming a fairly large adult vocabulary, between 10,000 and 20,000 words, the very first word you type on a sheet of paper or in a Word document requires you to know why you didn't make 10,000 to 20,000 other choices.

When everything is possible, choosing can be impossible. In other words, limiting people's choices has proved incredibly useful. Market researchers credit the success of McDonald's to this fact. The core of a McDonald's menu for decades was one thing—a hamburger—embedded in a few insignificant choices like ketchup or no ketchup, onions or no onions, a Big Mac or a Quarter Pounder. Having a choice makes people feel in control, even when most of our everyday choices are insignificant.

But reducing your choices to a manageable few is the very opposite of the attitude of abundance. Less isn't more. Yoga rescues us from this dilemma by a single powerful teaching: Creative intelligence organizes everything for you. It doesn't flow through you like water gushing through a garden hose or down a canyon ravine. If you align yourself with creative intelligence, it effortlessly organizes thoughts, words, and actions from a deeper level than the surface of the mind, which is where the random play of thoughts is so haphazard and unpredictable.

THE SEVEN CHAKRAS

Creative intelligence follows a path that brings out its seven qualities. The tradition of Yoga provides a flowchart that shows seven *Chakras*, taken from the Sanskrit word for wheel or circle. Chakras are arranged along the spinal column, but they exist in awareness, and are not part of your physical anatomy. Here is an illustration.

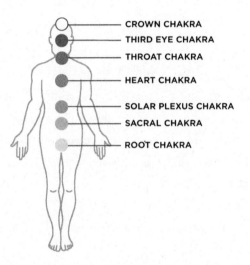

Yoga thus maps the flow of creative intelligence as it moves through you, expressing a different quality at each chakra, from top to bottom.

- Crown chakra: Bliss

- Forehead or third eye chakra: Intelligence

- Throat chakra: Self-expression

- Heart chakra: Love

- Solar plexus chakra: Successful action, self-empowerment

- Sacral chakra: Sexual pleasure, sensuality

- Root chakra: Security, safety

You can use the seven chakras in two ways. The first way is to strengthen each quality associated with a chakra. For instance, meditating on the crown chakra strengthens bliss while meditating on the heart chakra strengthens all emotions, but especially love. If you wanted a sense of inner security and safety, meditating on the root chakra, which grounds awareness in the physical world, would be appropriate.

BASIC CHAKRA MEDITATION

If you want to strengthen a quality of creative intelligence, there is a specific mantra for each one. They are simple but are derived from a deep source—the seers or rishis heard these sounds when they focused on each chakra.

Crown chakra: So hum (pronounced so *hum*), or simple awareness

Forehead/third eye chakra: Om (pronounced *ohm*)

Throat chakra: Ham (pronounced *hum*)

Heart chakra: Yam (pronounced *yum*)

Solar plexus chakra: Ram (pronounced *rahm*)

Sacral chakra: Vam (pronounced *vum*)

Root chakra: Lam (pronounced *lum*)

These so-called seed mantras are the basic vibration of each chakra in the form of a sound—sometimes there are general meanings (*So hum,* for example, means "I am" in Sanskrit), but they are not the intention of the mantra. The usual explanation is that repeating the mantra balances the energy that each chakra expresses. You don't have to adopt any beliefs about these issues, because the value of mantra meditation is already well established through thousands of research studies.

HOW TO MEDITATE

Choosing any mantra you want to meditate with, here is the basic method.

- Find a quiet time of day, the best usually being in the morning or afternoon.
- Sit quietly with your back upright, hands in your lap. (You don't have to sit in a traditional lotus posture, but don't lean back or lounge. Sitting upright in any way you find comfortable will work.)
- Close your eyes and take a few deep breaths until you feel calm and quiet inside.
- Place your attention in the location of the mantra you chose.

Crown chakra: Top of the head

Forehead/third eye chakra: Midpoint of the forehead, slightly above the eyes

Throat chakra: Middle of the throat, or larynx

Heart chakra: Center of the chest

Solar plexus chakra: Between the navel and the bottom of the rib cage

Sacral chakra: Two inches above the pelvic bone

Root chakra: Base of the spine

- Silently say the mantra and repeat it regularly, but not in a fixed rhythm. Just easily repeat the mantra in a relaxed way, and return to it if you notice that you have been distracted by other thoughts or sensations. (Note: For the crown chakra, you can do this without a mantra and sit in simple awareness.)
- Meditate with the mantra for ten to twenty minutes. Then sit quietly with your eyes closed for a few minutes. Lying down and resting for these few minutes is best, but if you don't have the time, just sit quietly to ease out of the meditative state before returning to your daily activity.

This basic meditation technique is one of the most effective for reaching deeper levels of awareness. Do not force yourself to focus on the chakra; do not attempt to concentrate. The opposite is what you want, a relaxed meditation that takes advantage of the mind's natural tendency to seek its source.

INTENTIONAL MEDITATION

You can also meditate on the quality of creative intelligence expressed by the chakra. This is meditation on a desire or intention, rather than a vibration. My term for them is "centering thoughts," because they bring your attention to the quiet center where intentions are most effective.

Crown chakra: "I am" or "I am pure Being."

Forehead/third eye chakra: "I know" or "I am knowingness."

Throat chakra: "I am free expression" or "I speak my truth."

Heart chakra: "I am love" or "I radiate love."

Solar plexus chakra: "I am in my power" or "I am empowerment."

Sacral chakra: "I am sensual" or "I embrace desire."

Root chakra: "I am always safe and secure" or "I am totally grounded."

Unlike meditating on a mantra, meditating on an intention means that you identify with the thought and believe it completely. Naturally, this isn't going to happen simply through repetition. The method is more intuitive, as follows:

- Sit quietly with your eyes closed and center yourself, as described for mantra meditation.
- Choose a centering thought and say it silently to yourself, just once.
- Let the meaning settle in your awareness and note what happens next. You might hear words, recall a memory, or feel a sensation. You don't

need to do anything with the response except to
notice it and let it rise and subside.
- Repeat the centering thought again, just once.
Wait for the next response, whatever it is.
Continue for ten to twenty minutes.
- Sit quietly for a few minutes or lie down, as
described for mantra meditation.

You will notice that all kinds of things can happen as
you meditate on your chosen thought. Think of these responses like layers of an onion. Each layer separates you
from the heart of the onion, and they must peel away to
reveal the heart.

Simple awareness melts away these veils or layers of
separation. Let's suppose you are meditating on "I am
love." You say this to yourself, and each time you get a
new response, for example:

You have the thought "I am not love," a form of
resistance.
Your attention goes to your heart. This either feels
good, neutral, or not so good.
You remember your first love, or you remember your
first breakup.

These responses separate you from truly believing
"I am love." Don't dwell on them. They will melt away
into silence, and, as they do, you will be drawn more and
more deeply in the silence. At some point you will think
"I am love," and it will be totally believable. It feels like
the real you, or your true self.

Don't expect to reach the goal the first time or every time you meditate. Your unconscious mind is dynamic and changeable. It has all kinds of reactions, but that isn't your concern. You are using the centering thought to settle more deeply into simple awareness, and, as you do, you will feel the presence of your true self. It is drawing you to it by a kind of subtle magnetic force, known in Sanskrit as *Swarupa*, the charm of being your true self.

Your true self has exerted this subtle attraction your whole life, and you experience glimpses of the qualities named in the centering thoughts. We have all had moments of intense peace or love, a feeling of belonging and being totally safe. Using the chakra system, you can strengthen your connection to your true self. Each quality of creative intelligence will expand and become more a part of you.

Meditation is the first important use of the chakras. The second is evolution, or inner growth. You seek to use creative intelligence in activity, as your day unfolds. This path takes advantage of a key aspect of consciousness: It is evolutionary by nature. It wants to expand, progress, deepen, and find new ways to express itself. In other living creatures, evolution is chiefly physical, and adaptions are narrowly focused on survival, finding enough food, and mating.

Only in *Homo sapiens* is evolution open-ended. We choose our own evolutionary path, one person at a time. The benefits might spread collectively, the way electricity and the combustion engine now dominate life everywhere. But these physical products began in consciousness. Yoga would say that a new invention requires certain qualities of creative intelligence, especially a bright idea or a sudden insight (sixth chakra, the center of intelligence), an excited feeling about making the discovery (fourth chakra, where emotions are centered), and the action needed to bring the invention to fruition (third chakra, where powerful action is centered).

Every quality of creative intelligence contains the possibility to become stronger, to renew itself in unexpected ways, and to carry you into areas of yourself where you want to grow. The flow of creative intelligence makes all of this possible without struggle. You follow the natural process of consciousness unfolding within itself.

In the following pages, I'll present the evolutionary possibilities for each chakra in detail. Infinite possibilities no longer need to feel overwhelming, and you don't need any longer to diminish your prospects to just a handful of manageable experiences. A vision of abundance should rest on unlimited possibilities, and the chakra system can organize each level of life where lasting fulfillment is achievable, so let's begin.

CHAKRA 7

The Source of Bliss

SEVENTH CHAKRA

Location: *Top of the head*

Theme: *Bliss*

Desirable qualities:

Blissfulness, joy, ecstasy

Oneness

Wholeness

The crown chakra is the center of bliss, which in Sanskrit is *Ananda*. When you enliven the crown chakra, you are connected to the very source of bliss. The tradition of Yoga teaches that consciousness is blissful in it-self. You do not need an outside stimulus—a beautiful sunset, playing with a baby, eating a chocolate truffle—to trigger bliss. Such pleasures come and go, but your connection to bliss at the source is constant and ever-present. The only requirement is that you exist.

Since we already exist, what's the point of the crown chakra? In the lore of Yoga, this is where the soul exits at death or at the moment of liberation when a yogi is enlightened. That event is not a death but a kind of departure, transcending the body to enter and merge with pure awareness. When you are enlightened, you are united with Being or, in common parlance, "I am" drops the "I," leaving only the "Am."

Glimpses of joy and blissful moments are not adequate to really get your arms around Ananda. Every process that keeps creation going, including your body's cells, the environment, billions of species of micro-organisms, and even the vibration of atoms and molecules, are manifesta-tions of Ananda. Yet despite its cosmic scale, we have to start here, at the source. In everyday life, Ananda is related to

> *Inspiration*
>
> *Spiritual impulses, seeking*
>
> *Feeling vibrant and alive*
>
> *Wakefulness*
>
> *Transcendence*
>
> *Lightness of being*

Taken together, these are the fundamentals of spirituality. Yoga inter-prets spirituality in terms of bliss-consciousness, rather than in terms of God and religious belief. If you enliven the crown chakra and experience the flow of bliss into your awareness, nothing is more evolutionary.

Ananda is an alien and exotic concept in the West. In modern India, there isn't much significance to the word, although many people know the formulation *Sat Chit Ananda*, translated as "eternal bliss-consciousness." This is the basic "stuff" of creation, starting not with "And on the first day God created," but with pure awareness bursting forth with the infinite creativity of Ananda. Putting Ananda at the heart of creation as a kind of cosmic vibratory force (not all that different from the vibrating quantum fields that generated the universe, according to modern physics) doesn't really help the average person. But Ananda got a lucky breakthrough, and it opens the way to the crown chakra in our journey through the seven chakras.

"FOLLOW YOUR BLISS"

Without uttering the word *Ananda*, the famous scholar of mythology Joseph Campbell brought it to the West in an acceptable form. He originated a phrase almost everyone knows by now: "Follow your bliss." With these words, Campbell found a new way to inspire people at the level of consciousness without them even knowing that he had consciousness in mind. ("Follow your bliss" first gained wide circulation through a 1988 public television interview with Bill Moyers. You can view it on YouTube by searching JOSEPH CAMPBELL BLISS.)

He held out a vision that was radically different from the notion that hard work, persistence, and keeping your shoulder to the grindstone were the keys to success. As Campbell explained, "Follow your bliss, don't be afraid, and doors will open where you didn't know they were going to be."

Campbell's advocacy of a blissful life had deep spiritual roots. He believed that these roots were inside everyone, and therein lay a secret. This is made clear when you read a bit more of his explanation. "If you do follow your bliss, you put yourself on a kind of track that has been there all the while, waiting for you." In other words, bliss allows you to step into the unknown without danger or risk. Unseen allies will rise up to help you. In Campbell's words, a huge transformation occurs when ". . . the life you ought to be living is the one you *are* living."

Pause and ask yourself, "What is the life I ought to be living?" Almost everyone will come up with an answer they received secondhand. Single out the word *ought*. We all come from formative backgrounds. Influenced by a strict upbringing, some people believe that *ought* means doing your duty, following the rules, and standing for moral values. Someone living in an age of faith would be certain that *ought* means obeying God's laws. A carefree child plays and laughs without worries, so, for her, *ought* means doing whatever a person feels like doing or whatever you can get away with until a scolding parent intervenes. So, in our own way, each of us has a preconceived notion of the life we ought to be leading, and the models we follow are handed down by family and society, heroes and role models.

Moreover, it might not even be desirable to follow your bliss. Should you quit your job as an accountant, office manager, or salesperson and jump immediately into opera singing, painting, or raising roses because that's what you really love? Normal life would be disrupted if everyone ran around doing only the things they loved. But that is how most people interpreted Campbell's explanation.

In the end, "Follow your bliss" needs to be clarified to rid it of confusion and contradictions. "Be in your dharma" is not as catchy, but it encompasses more of what Campbell was getting at. We've come that far in this book already, but there is more to say about how bliss-consciousness makes possible every other value of love, creativity, intelligence, and the rest that flow through the chakras. Moments of joy tell you that you can feel blissful. They cannot tell you that you have bliss-consciousness as your source.

"I AM ENOUGH"

Yoga's approach to life is based on consciousness, and consciousness has only two states. It can be moving or not moving. If Einstein is thinking about relativity, Mozart is composing a symphony, or Shakespeare is writing a sonnet, consciousness is moving. This state is familiar to everyone. But think about Einstein, Mozart, and Shakespeare taking a nap. Now consciousness isn't moving. But this apparent stasis, where nothing is happening in the mind, doesn't alter who they are. A sleeping genius is still a genius. All the potential remains, but it hasn't been activated.

This simple example turns out to be of tremendous importance. If you look at yourself and how your life is going, the things that are most valuable to you have been parceled out—you have only so much and no more of love, intelligence, creativity, success, and so on. Everything you've achieved has happened when consciousness was moving. But the aspect of consciousness that isn't moving is your source, and it is infinite. Bliss-consciousness isn't an experience in its non-moving state. It is like a reservoir from which you draw love, intelligence, creativity, and the like.

It isn't necessary to be a genius in order to have access to this limitless reservoir—but it is necessary to know that it exists. To switch metaphors, if you need a new car but have only a small bank account, your choices will be limited. But if you have millions in the bank, your choices are much wider. For various reasons you might wind up buying the same economy model as the person with much less money, but it makes all the difference to know that your reserve is there. If you have an abundance of money in the bank, in the back of your mind you know you will always have enough money, which is far different from someone who knows he lacks money.

Now let's translate this into your situation right now. Set aside anything you might be thinking, feeling, saying, or doing. At the level where your awareness isn't moving, either you feel "I am enough" or you feel "I am not enough." The difference is your connection to your source. This is what makes the crown chakra so important, because it is the place where the connection is made. Before bliss-consciousness enters the active mind, it establishes you as completely whole. Wholeness expresses itself in the silent knowledge of "I am enough."

A famous South Indian guru, Nisargadatta Maharaj, explained this by means of a metaphor. A disciple asked Nisargadatta how he knew he was enlightened, and here is his response: "I am like flour. All kinds of things can be made from flour—bread, noodles, every kind of baked goods. But I am not any of those things. I am the flour itself, and no matter what my mind is doing, I remain certain that I am pure consciousness." In the *Bhagavad Gita*, Lord Krishna expresses the same thing, speaking not as an enlightened being or a god, but as the Self: "It cannot be cut with weapons, burned by fire, made wet with water, or dried by air."

These are metaphors for wholeness, which isn't affected by change. Yoga teaches that wholeness isn't something you strive for. You can change your diet so it contains whole foods; you can change your doctor to one who practices holistic methods. But you cannot change yourself to become whole. You are whole already and haven't realized it yet. In the *Gita,* Lord Krishna defines wisdom in a single axiom: "I am the field and the knower of the field."

Field can mean many things, from the battlefield (Krishna is advising the warrior Arjuna on the eve of battle) or the quantum field, whose vibrations and ripples give rise to the physical universe. You can learn about any field and become "the knower of the field." But supreme knowledge comes when you can say, "My field is consciousness." Only then are you the knower of reality itself.

All of these understandings get compressed into "I am enough," which is the ultimate expression of abundance. You place consciousness in its pure, unmoving state before consciousness is on the move.

"I AM NOT ENOUGH"

If you do the opposite and rely on the active mind and everything that it produces—thinking, feeling, speaking, and doing—you will never know what it is like to be whole. Your life will become a story, filled with good and bad events, good and bad memories, good and bad impulses. Building a story is what everyone does. It comes naturally to the ego personality, whose agenda is to focus on "I, me, and mine." If you are fortunate and have made good choices, you are likely to be happy with your story so far. It helps to have an advantage before you start, such as being white, male, born to money, and living in a prosperous society.

But no matter how good your story is, it will be based on an agenda devised by your ego. This agenda is based on several familiar motives:

The Ego's Agenda

- Get more of what you want.

- Look good in the eyes of others.

- Hide your guilty side.

- Paper over old wounds and hurts.

- Don't repeat bad experiences from the past.

- Defend yourself from possible threats.

- Form a close circle of family and friends while excluding others.

- Never look at your deepest fears, including fear of death.

Taken together, the ego's agenda is based on "I am not enough." There is no connection to the infinite reservoir of consciousness. Instead, there is a constant stream of either/or choices:

- Either I like it or it turns me off.

- Either I want it or I don't want it.

- Either it fits my lifestyle or it doesn't.

- Either it improves my self-image or it makes me look bad.

It would seem as if this way of approaching life comes naturally and is the right way to live: Create the best story you can by making the best choices. Madison Avenue thrives by presenting the consumer with choices that tease us into thinking that newer, better, and best—in shampoos, vacuum cleaners, frozen pizzas, or luxury cars—will boost our self-image.

Yet operating from the ego's agenda has a strong undertow, which is why it leads to frustration and dissatisfaction for millions of people, no matter how hard they try. The nagging sense of "I am not enough" is the undertow. But hardly anyone is willing to step out of their ego's agenda. The reasons are traceable to very common rationalizations:

- I don't want to be different.

- Things have to get better—they always do.

- I just need to be more disciplined.

- I just need to work harder.

- I refuse to admit failure.

These whispers from your ego keep you in line. One way or another, they keep everyone in line, even the microscopic sliver of the population who are the stars of Hollywood, rock music, and Wall Street, and those appearing on the cover of *People* magazine.

ACTIVATING THE CROWN CHAKRA

Once they are told about the undertow in the ego's agenda, most reasonable people would want a solution. The solution, according to Yoga, is to activate the crown chakra, because it connects you to the reservoir of bliss-consciousness. A few things have been covered in general terms already:

- Be in simple awareness. When you notice that you aren't, take a few minutes to center yourself.
- Meditate on the mantra *So hum* (page 84).
- Meditate on the centering thought "I am" or "I am pure Being" (page 87).

Other steps are more specifically aimed at activating the crown chakra. Since this chakra is the center of bliss-consciousness, so are the steps you can take to activate it. Reflect on the following suggestions and adopt the ones you feel most comfortable with first.

Bliss-consciousness is *generous*, so take every opportunity to show generosity in your own life. Generosity of spirit is more important than being generous with your money. When you are generous of spirit you show respect for everyone. You support their best impulses without criticizing their worst. You are gracious and sympathetic. You open your heart whenever you can, helping the other person feel accepted.

Bliss-consciousness is *giving*, so take every opportunity to give of yourself. The ego's agenda revolves around taking, which only reinforces the attitude of "I am not enough." You give from a sense of overflowing abundance. As one yogic metaphor puts it, you are like a tree laden with fruit whose branches bend to earth so everyone can pick the fruit. The most valuable thing you can give is your undivided attention, but there is also appreciation and acceptance to give, and they have their own rewards.

Bliss-consciousness is *inspiring*, so find a source of inspiration and go to it every day. It can be inspiring poetry or music, the scriptures of a spiritual tradition, or listening to your inner inspiration in order to make something beautiful. There is great value in finding someone who needs to be inspired and uplifting them any way you can.

BREATHING EXERCISE

Yoga prescribes many kinds of controlled breathing, and these are often part of a hatha yoga class. Here is a simple exercise that uses both breath and visuals. Its purpose is to see and feel the path that bliss-consciousness traces as it travels through you.

- Sit upright in a quiet place with your eyes closed.
- Breathe naturally. As you inhale, see white light moving from your heart out through the top of your head. As you exhale, see white light descending through your body and out the soles of your feet.
- Don't force your breathing into a fixed rhythm, and if you lose track of the imaging while breathing, that's quite all right.
- Continue for five minutes, then sit quietly in simple awareness.

CHAKRA 6

Highest Intelligence

SIXTH CHAKRA

Location: Forehead / third eye

Theme: Intelligence

Desirable qualities:

Knowingness

Insight

Intuition

Imagination

The theme of the sixth chakra is intelligence, an unparalleled attainment in *Homo sapiens*. This is symbolically where bliss-consciousness transforms itself into the mind with its constant stream of thoughts, perceptions, reason, and intellect. In the modern world, those functions have created an endless supply of technology and scientific breakthroughs. But the same powers of reason have veered into creativity that is diabolical in its destructive power.

In creating nuclear weapons, biochemical weapons, and ever-more-sophisticated methods to bring about mass death, reason is responsible for horrors that we never seem to escape. Every new weapon seems reasonable to those who devise and use it. With these realities, one of the most basic tenets of Yoga has been betrayed: Evolution—in other words, the progress of consciousness—is the track everyone should be on. If success is measured by bliss, how can the destructive aspects of reason be anything but a slide backward? Taking perfectly reasonable actions did more than create the horror of modern warfare. The use of fossil fuels and the internal combustion engine were triumphs of progress until the damage they caused the environment was tragically revealed.

In order for the sixth chakra to be activated, "intelligence" must include the subtler ways the mind works, through intuition, insight, and imagination. Yoga places more importance on them than on rationality, because your mind has to tell you when a perfectly reasonable idea has destructive undertones. We can bring this to the personal level very easily. Anyone who has made wrong choices in a relationship partner typically wails, "If I had only seen what he was really like" or "When she told me she wanted to break up, I was blindsided." Having an intuitive grasp of the relationship from the beginning would have helped, and when you are connected to dharma, there is no need to think through any personal issues, including relationships. Creative intelligence has a quality that guides you from within, *knowingness*, which is centered in the sixth chakra.

If you activate this chakra, you have opened the "third eye," which refers to these subtler powers (there is no physical third eye, however). There's a commonly shared belief that intuition is real, but in Yoga belief isn't the issue. What matters is whether you can trust your flashes of intuition, hunches, and gut feelings—all the subtle mental impulses that totally rational people (as they see themselves) are skeptical of.

Some people trust their intuition enough that they keep their antennas out, looking for indications that most people are insensitive to. (There's even a descriptive name, "a sensitive," for the highly intuitive.) In general, however, relying on the subtler powers of the mind has drastically declined. Modern people are far removed from ancient cultures that believed in oracles, looked upon dreams as prophecy, or felt a divine presence emanating from saints and holy relics. Great civilizations rose through the potency of this worldview, which connected humans with the timeless.

Obviously, the road back isn't to abandon our own modern worldview but to expand reality. If you consider reason the most important guide to life, as a scientist probably would, your powers of reason are real and will grow. If you believe that intuition is just as important as reason, it will be real to you and will grow. The ideal is to have both aspects in your life. It is true, according to neuroscience, that either the right or the left side of the brain dominates in us. This was popularized as "left-brain people" (who are rational, problem-solving, and logical) and "right-brain people" (who are creative, intuitive, and artistic). But both hemispheres of the brain complement and coordinate with each other.

Yoga is a whole-brain approach or, more accurately, a whole-mind approach. Intuition isn't gained by shutting out or ignoring reason but by finding a subtler level of the mind. After all, a mathematician can be highly creative—this is one of the highest compliments you can give in advanced mathematics, when someone comes up with a solution no one has seen before. You can also have a musical mind, like Johann Sebastian Bach's, which was unparalleled for organizing notes in the complex configurations known as counterpoint.

A WHOLE-MIND SURVEY

Creative intelligence nurtures the whole mind, but, as time passes, we all develop our own quirks, which turn into a mind-set. We see ourselves as logical and reasonable, in which case artists and "creative types" are different enough from us that we tend to be suspicious of them. A mind-set in the other direction, toward the completely intuitive, might lift you so far into the clouds that you have no use for "left-brain types."

But a mind-set is rarely this cut-and-dried. To see how much you favor one side over the other, place a check mark by each of following statements if you feel that it applies to you.

LOGICAL / RATIONAL MIND

—— I approach tasks methodically.

—— I keep my work space neat and tidy.

—— I read articles on science, technology, medicine, or finance.

—— I am good at fixing things around the house.

—— I would be comfortable tutoring a schoolchild in math.

—— I took physics, chemistry, or math in college.

—— I like puzzles and mental games.

—— I believe that science is the best approach to solving difficult problems.

___ I believe that it will take technology to solve the climate crisis.

___ I think scientists will one day create an intelligent computer equal to human intelligence.

___ I think the key to consciousness lies in the brain.

___ In my personal relationship, I am the more rational one.

Score: (0–12)

INTUITIVE / CREATIVE MIND

___ I think of myself as creative.

___ I have a good instinct for what people are really like.

___ I tend to invent my own recipes rather than follow a cookbook.

___ I can paint, dance, or play a musical instrument.

___ I can feel the mood in a room as soon as I walk into it.

___ I am quick to notice another person's moods.

___ I am absolutely against violence.

___ I make impulse purchases and don't regret them.

___ I am a warm parent.

___ I read articles about the arts.

___ I am inspired by poetry or scriptures.

___ I have a childlike side.

Score: _____ (0–12)

ASSESSING YOUR SCORE

If your score skewed sharply toward Logical / Rational or Intuitive / Creative, you have a strong mind-set. Once they settle into a mind-set, people tend to stick to it, and your behavior has a strong tendency in that direction. A maximum score for each section is twelve, and if you are near the maximum, you identify with your mind-set. It is your worldview for all practical purposes. If your score on the *other* section is four or less, you might tend to ignore or be intolerant of someone with a mind-set opposite to yours.

If your score is fairly balanced for both sections, you are not strongly attached to your mind-set. You make room for logic, order, and method, but you also make room for hunches, creativity, and inspiration.

If you scored nine or higher in *both* sections, you are a rare person indeed. Rather than fixing on one mind-set, you combine the best of rationality and intuition. In Yoga, you would be seen as very attuned to the flow of creative intelligence, which nurtures both sides of the mind.

If you scored five or lower on both sections, you either resisted being asked these questions or were in too much of a rush to fully reflect on them.

BYPASSING YOUR MIND-SET

Being attached to your mind-set can be a great advantage. It provides a sharp focus on science and technology if your mind-set is Rational / Logical, makes you methodical and organized, and can lead to a satisfying career as an accountant, a technician, a manager, and many other jobs people would call "left-brain." If you are strongly Intuitive / Creative, you will thrive in the arts or any creative endeavor, like cooking and decorating. You will feel satisfied with a lifestyle that gives you freedom to express yourself, follow your intuition, and bond emotionally with others.

Yoga is about escaping your mind-set, however. A strong mind-set is lopsided, but that isn't the issue. The issue is being open to the flow of creative intelligence, which is marked by a mind that is open, flexible, not stuck in fixed beliefs, and capable of being constantly renewed through beauty, love, curiosity, discovery, and insight. In other words, your state of awareness is much more important than any mind-set, no matter how successful that mind-set might be.

Yoga teaches that awareness gives up nothing. Reason isn't diminished by intuition; intuition isn't undercut by reason. Your goal should be a whole mind, which is the truest and best definition of intelligence.

To escape your mind-set, certain steps will be familiar to you already from reading this book. Be in simple awareness. Take time to center yourself whenever you are stressed or distracted. Favor the behaviors that work toward success (see "How We Get Money Right," page 45) over those that don't (see "How We Get Money Wrong," page 43). But these steps alone won't enable you to see the value of escaping your mind-set, which has to come first.

What gives your mind its ultimate power is that it assigns meaning to raw experience. For example, think of the color red. Does it mean anything? In and of itself, no, because red is just a wavelength of light that happens to create a particular vibration in the cells of the retina at the back of your eye. But once the mind begins to work its magic, red becomes a symbol for all kinds of things: passion, anger, blood, danger, a message to stop your car at a stoplight or stop sign. "I see red" means you are enraged, yet a valentine with a red heart is a sign of love, and, in the symbolism of Roman Catholicism, the bleeding heart of Jesus indicates both compassion and great suffering. In the same way all the raw materials of life—everything you see, hear, touch, taste, and smell—has meaning because your mind gives it meaning.

Having given meaning to a raw experience, you assign value to it automatically. You will know, for example, whether you would buy a red car or wear a red dress. By assigning value to your experiences over a lifetime, you have developed your mind-set. It has taken many years and thousands of separate experiences to create your own mind-set, all the way back to early childhood. A fixed mind-set is very difficult to change, particularly if you have had strong emotional-psychological experiences.

This lesson was forcefully brought home to me recently. I was told about Jeanne, a friend of a friend who lives in France. Jeanne is a teacher outside Paris and is very intelligent and capable. She seems liberal and open-minded except for one blind spot: Muslims. Jeanne is quick to spot any negative news stories about Muslims, particularly those who have immigrated to France.

After receiving some angry emails from Jeanne about how bad Muslims are, I called her out as politely as I could. She hotly replied that she was not prejudiced. Instead, she had personal experience to support her dislike of all Muslims.

It happened forty years ago when Jeanne was a young teacher at the French equivalent of junior high. A Muslim girl came to class wearing a headscarf. Seeing the glances the girl was getting from the other students, Jeanne took her aside and told her, in the most reasonable tones, that it would be better not to wear the headscarf to school. Without reply, the girl slapped Jeanne hard in the face and stalked off. Jeanne never forgot this incident, and to this day she holds all Muslims responsible for it. While some people could have written this incident off as rude and unpleasant—the action of one person taking Jeanne's well-meaning suggestion the wrong way—Jeanne saw it as something much deeper and insidious. It became a permanent part of her mind-set toward Muslims in general.

A mind-set is the product of experiences that aren't all traumatic, however. Mostly we remain unaware of how much they build up. A mind-set is much like a coral reef built up by accumulating one tiny soft coral polyp at a time. You can't change such a massive construction overnight.

Fortunately, you don't have to. What you need to do is much simpler. Bypass your mind-set altogether. A skeptic would mutter, "Easier said than done," and he would be right if we were prisoners of our mind-set. But we don't have to be. No matter how mechanically you respond to the same experiences that get repeated over and over, your mind isn't a machine. When using a desktop computer or your smartphone, there is a straight line between input and output. Ask Siri for today's weather, and the answer you get will be about the weather. Ask a person to tell you the weather, however, and any response is possible, including the following: "I don't know"; "Find out for yourself"; "Who cares about the weather?"; "Leave me alone"; "Go jump in the lake." When talking to another person, there is no guarantee that you'll get the answer you seek.

Computers are wired for logic. You are wired for receptivity to a huge range of experiences, and you receive these experiences on either a closed or an open channel. It isn't part of the setup that you should respond with fear, prejudice, or a closed mind. Those are all self-created parts of the ego, in its posture of self-defense. By shutting out whatever is different or unexpected, the ego builds walls that are completely fictitious—at a deeper level of awareness, you still are keenly aware of everything that is happening to you.

KNOWINGNESS

Ironically, this is how awareness got a bad reputation. "What I don't know can't hurt me" is false. "Ignorance is bliss" offers exactly the wrong definition of bliss. Yet many people try to know as little as possible about perceived threats, and, in the bargain, they lose awareness of life itself. They are fated to be unconscious most of the time and suspicious of becoming more aware, because they assume that knowing too much is painful. This is, in essence, a repudiation of creative intelligence.

It is your own personal choice whether to learn everything you can about a medical condition or an upcoming surgery, but that's not the issue. The sixth chakra is about *knowingness*, which is a state of awareness, not a set of facts and information. In the *Bhagavad Gita*, Lord Krishna declares, "I am the field and the knower of the field." The word *field* has three meanings. First is the field of activity, represented in this instance by a battlefield, since the *Gita* takes place on the eve of battle. A knower of the field would be a warrior like Arjuna, who is listening to the discourse, from Lord Krishna, in the guise of his charioteer.

The second field is the body, and by inhabiting a physical body we are all knowers of what it is like to experience pain and pleasure. But the third field is more important, because it is the field of consciousness. Lord Krishna's teaching, which is pure Yoga, is that wisdom only comes to the knower of this field. Those who know only the field of activity and the experience of being in a physical body are deluded or, to be more tactful, they are misled. They are judging life from the level of physical and mental activity, whereas wisdom comes from the source.

It is baffling, then, to consider a famous remark attributed by Plato to his mentor Socrates: "All I know is that I know nothing." Why did a philosopher renowned for wisdom say this? It makes Socrates seem to be anti-knowledge. In fact, the kind of knowledge Socrates opposed was specious knowledge. His philosophical antagonists, the Sophists, taught the better class of young men in Athens, and what they transmitted, if we translate it into modern terms, was that wisdom can be passed on from teacher to pupil. What Socrates taught was intuitive inner knowing. "All I know is that I know nothing" refers to a state of awareness where there is nothing to know, because knowingness is innate in everyone.

If you align yourself with the flow of creative intelligence, you will emerge with successful thoughts. But they are secondary products. First and foremost is your state of awareness. The more you rely on a mind-set, the more disconnected you will be from your inner knowingness. This is what the great English novelist D. H. Lawrence was getting at when he wrote, "All that we know is nothing, we are merely crammed wastepaper baskets, unless we are in touch with that which laughs at all our knowing."

BECOME A CONSCIOUS THINKER

In any field, the most successful thinkers have one thing in common: They think for themselves. They don't fall prey to secondhand beliefs. They aren't overly influenced by anyone else's opinions. Old conditioning doesn't dominate their thinking process.

How well do you think for yourself? This is a crucial question, and it's worthwhile giving yourself a clear answer, which you can do by taking the following quiz.

QUIZ

Do You Think for Yourself?

Answer the following fifteen questions by checking either *Agree* or *Disagree*. If in doubt, think about your past rather than what you happen to think right this minute.

In general I want to please.

Agree ☐   **Disagree** ☐

I have voted for the same political party all my life.

Agree ☐   **Disagree** ☐

I don't like to be picked out and noticed.

Agree ☐   **Disagree** ☐

I believe that if you can't say something good about somebody, say nothing at all.

Agree ☐   **Disagree** ☐

I am not a leader and don't want to be.

Agree ☐   **Disagree** ☐

I'm not all that special.

Agree ☐   **Disagree** ☐

People don't think I'm an oddball.

Agree ☐   **Disagree** ☐

Rather than argue, I will keep my opinions to myself.

Agree ☐   **Disagree** ☐

Not much about my life inspires me.

Agree ☐   **Disagree** ☐

It is important to take one for the team.

Agree ☐   **Disagree** ☐

No one really considers me a mentor or role model.

Agree ☐   **Disagree** ☐

Sensible goals are better than wild dreams that will never come true.

Agree ☐   **Disagree** ☐

Our family mostly sees things the same way.

Agree ☐   Disagree ☐

Hard mental challenges intimidate me.

Agree ☐   Disagree ☐

I'm no expert.

Agree ☐   Disagree ☐

Total: Agree = _____   Disagree = _____

ASSESSING YOUR SCORE

Thinking for yourself is the opposite of being a conformist. If you marked Agree ten times or more, you are unusually conformist. If you marked Disagree ten times or more, you are unusually nonconformist. These are not value judgments. They point to unconscious beliefs and assumptions about how life works.

We all have a mixture of conformist and nonconformist inside us, so most scores will be fairly evenly divided between *Agree* and *Disagree*. We sometimes think for ourselves, yet we sometimes go along to get along, too. Unless you value nonconformity, however, you can't really think for yourself. Your inner programming prevents you from doing so, in subtle and not-so-subtle ways. One person might associate nonconformity with social activism, protest, being a crank or oddball, while someone else might associate nonconformity with radically new thinking by a Newton or an Einstein.

It becomes a struggle to value yourself as an original when the tug of conformity makes you fear being *too* original. You might have heard of the tall poppy syndrome, the practice of shaming people for standing out from the crowd. An online article describes the syndrome this way: "It is often said that Australians tend to cut tall poppies down to size by denigrating them. It may have its origin in an obsolete 17th-century sense of the word *poppy*, meaning 'a conspicuous or prominent person or thing, frequently with implication of likely humiliation.'"

What really matters is to be free of framing things as the tall poppy who might be cut down or as the egotist who must stand out from the crowd. Either way, unconscious drives are in control. It is important, no matter whether anyone else approves or disapproves, to know that you are an original.

It makes life simpler if you rely on automatic thinking. You have ready-made answers, opinions, beliefs, and judgments. But life is dynamic. It is constantly changing in ways that no longer fit automatic responses.

We program our own minds and also let outside forces program our minds for us. Both processes are at work all the time. The most powerful agent for self-programming is the ego. Individual life is built around "my family," "my job," "my likes and dislikes." Yet when you gaze at the sky, you don't say, "my sky" or "my blue." The sea isn't "my ocean," no matter how close you live to it. The experience is universal.

In subtle form, your ego is much more limiting that you realize. "I" isn't an innocent word. Behind it lies a selfish agenda. Following the ego agenda, you might wind up thinking like this:

- I matter more than the other people here.

- What I have to say is important.

- I look out for number one.

- Winning is what matters. Being a loser is intolerable.

- I won't be satisfied until I've climbed to the top.

- Competition is Darwinian: Only the fittest survive.

Are these the thoughts of a highly competitive, successful person who should serve as a role model or the thoughts of a psychopath, who is devoid of guilt? The line is almost too fine to draw, which is why psychologists often point out how close to psychopathology many famous leaders are. (The French biologist and philosopher Jean Rostand declared, "Kill one man, and you are a murderer. Kill millions of men, and you are a conqueror. Kill them all, and you are a god.")

Each of us has an invisible box where we gather all the elements of the ego, and without being pathological, we go there to fetch thoughts to bolster I, me, and mine. Pause for a moment to reflect on the automatic thinking that is the product of ego.

Your Ego Is Thinking for You Whenever . . .

- You try to impress other people, even strangers.

- You insist on being right.

- You won't drop an argument until you win it, or the other person gives up.

- You are subject to flattery.

- You crave the approval of others.

- You always speak up at a meeting, even when you don't have much to say or everybody is tired.

- You ignore those who are in need.

- You look for ways to act dominant.

- You have an air of superiority.

- You consider your opinion the most important opinion in the room.

- You look upon competitors as personal enemies.

- You assume that you are doing more to carry your relationship than your partner.

- You demand that your children reflect well upon you.

- You withhold your attention, appreciation, and even sex to punish someone else.

This list's purpose isn't to make you feel bad about yourself but to indicate how pervasive the ego agenda is, and how everyday behavior follows this agenda in small and large ways. The ego isn't necessarily at fault—a strong sense of self is valuable, and all children must develop a sense of self, weak or strong, to navigate through life. The fault lies in letting your ego become a separate entity, a voice in your head, that you take no responsibility for. The excesses of ego are entirely mind-made. They are the consequences of self-programming.

The other major source of automatic thinking is social programming. Society has its own agenda, or rather a whole set of agendas. When you fall back on any social agenda, you put others first. But this selflessness is a bit of a red herring. Acquiescing to a group or tribe looks innocent enough at first sight, and the automatic thinking that results often makes your life easier. It feels modest and unassuming to have thoughts like the following:

- It takes teamwork to accomplish anything important, and there is no "I" in team.

- The more support you have, the more likely you are to succeed.

- We all need to pull together when the going gets tough.

- Nothing is more important than family.

- I'm not cut out to be a hero.

- Getting along will solve a lot of problems.

- Society is about law and order.

These thoughts are the product of social conditioning, beginning in early childhood. From the first day a parent told you what to do, you have encountered people you obey, follow, imitate, admire, feel loyal to, and consider better than yourself (however you want to define *better*). The problem, as with the ego agenda, is that blindly following the social agenda leads to excesses. Pause for a moment and consider if following the social agenda has programmed you in unwanted ways.

Society Is Thinking for You Whenever . . .

- You go along to get along.

- You engage in us-versus-them thinking.

- You are afraid to rock the boat.

- You turn a blind eye when your people do something wrong.

- You support a political leader out of partisan loyalty, no matter how flawed he is.

- You privately believe that people of color are inferior.

- You put your race, religion, political party, and nationality first.

- You protect a family member from the police, even though you know they are guilty.

- You automatically support any war your country enters.

- You regard protesters as troublemakers.

- You support the police, no matter what.

- You are a rabid sports fanatic.

- You find it hard to speak your truth.

- You support corporations over the interest of the individual.

- You go whichever way the wind blows.

Because the social agenda takes in large groups of people—unlike the ego agenda, which concerns only one person—these excesses can lead to ghastly results. The worst wars are the product of nationalism; horrific treatment of minorities is based on us-versus-them thinking. Programmed by the social agenda, a populace that blindly follows a Hitler, a Stalin, or a Mao is bolstered by knowing, in their heart of hearts, that they are doing the right and moral thing. Followers of authoritarian leaders don't change their minds after the leader's cruelty and unlawfulness have been exposed. If anything, a follower's loyalty is likely to grow stronger the more excessive the leader is.

Of course, the average person's behavior is generally within socially acceptable limits, but a programmed mind is still a programmed mind. Most people aren't concerned about deprogramming their minds. They are more apt to fall into the ego agenda or social agenda according to how it suits their temperament. One of these agendas and not the other controls the reactions that people display without thinking. Consider the following examples:

- At the airport a flight cancellation has been announced. One person grumbles, "This can't be happening to me. I have someplace really important to get to." Another person says, "I'll just sit tight. They'll straighten this out."

- A kindergarten teacher calls to inform a mother that Johnny is beating up on the weaker children and making them cry. One mother says, "Not my child. You've got it wrong." Another mother says, "I'm so sorry. We have to get to the bottom of this."

- A managerial position opens up at work. One coworker says, "I deserve this promotion. No one is better qualified." Another coworker says, "I can improve my chances by coming to work early and doing a better job."

In each example, the first person is following the ego agenda, the second person the social agenda. Finding a middle ground isn't easy, because the assumptions behind each agenda are so divergent. This is why so many people simply accept a mind-set without question. It creates stress when you are torn between two competing forces—personal and social. Shakespeare's plays are filled with such conflicts. Romeo loves Juliet, but their two families hate each other. Hamlet knows that there is something rotten in the state of Denmark, but he cries out in anguish, "O cursed spite, that ever I was born to set it right!" Julius Caesar's dying words, "*Et tu, Brute*," accuse a friend of the ultimate disloyalty, conspiring with the enemy.

Beyond the realm of tragedy, the lesson here is that *automatic thinking is never successful thinking*. Once you realize this, you have taken a crucial step toward thinking for yourself. But we need to draw much closer to creative intelligence. It alone allows you to be a successful thinker in any situation. In the most fundamental way, what creative intelligence gives you is wisdom. In effect, wisdom *is* creative intelligence.

The Anatomy of Wisdom

- An open mind

- Flexible responses

- Clear perceptions

- Unclouded thinking

- Lack of bias

- Positive expectations

This is where creative intelligence is much more effective than routine thinking. Pause and consider your experience in high school math class. The teacher presents the day's lesson, and then what? Some students will enjoy math, absorb it quickly, be open to new challenges, and feel confident that they will get a good grade. Other students feel bored or insecure about learning the lesson. A few might panic and carry this panic around for life. The difference between success and failure couldn't be more obvious, and yet we can't explain our own reactions to ourselves in a myriad of other experiences and encounters.

Sometimes we are open-minded, sometimes not. In certain situations, we have positive expectations; in other situations, we fear the worst. There's every reason to stop relying on this jumble of reactions. They are inconsistent and untrustworthy. With every negative situation, we reinforce our lack of confidence, our confusion, and our uncertainty. Biases get confirmed. The mind narrows.

Yet there are centuries of wisdom traditions that show us how to use creative intelligence to the fullest. The guiding principles are timeless. Here are the most important ones.

- Simple awareness is all you need.

- The mind has a level of awareness where solutions exist to every problem.

- Operate from this level of solution.

- Rely on creative intelligence—it permeates every aspect of life.

Simple awareness is a threshold experience. By giving your mind access to the flow of creative intelligence, you are aligning yourself with wisdom. True wisdom is dynamic and alive. Trusting in creative intelligence, you shift your mind away from any agenda based on ego or social conditioning. The whole point of a threshold is that something lies on the other side. In the chakra system, what lies on the other side is more transformation.

I haven't mentioned the chakras for a while, but by expanding on what *intelligence* really means in the light of Yoga, we've been dwelling in the area of the sixth chakra. Any attention you pay to the mind activates this chakra, but there are other things we can do to nurture awareness, which is the real key to higher intelligence in all its various forms.

ACTIVATING THE FOREHEAD / THIRD EYE CHAKRA

This chakra strengthens every aspect of mind but especially intuition, insight, and imagination. A few things you can do apply to every chakra in general:

- Be in simple awareness. When you notice that you aren't, take a few minutes to center yourself.

- Meditate on the mantra *Om* (page 84).
- Meditate on the centering thought "I know" or "I am knowingness" (page 87).

Other steps are more specifically aimed at activating the forehead chakra. The most important thing is to shift your awareness away from mental activity to the level of knowingness. You can accomplish this by developing your intuition, because knowingness is intuitive knowledge. Intuition is the ability to see what your eyes can't see. It can be experienced as direct knowledge without information. It can be insight and sudden flashes of certainty.

EXERCISE #1: DIRECT KNOWLEDGE

Intuition in its purest form is knowledge that you gain directly, without having to reason it out. Close your eyes and ask where a certain lost object is. See the object in question. See where it is now located, waiting until your mind gives you a clear image with details. Vague and fleeting images usually come from a desire not to fail at the exercise or reflect prior guesses and places where you've already looked.

If you don't get a strong visual image, ask to find the object as soon as possible; request that it be returned to you because you need it. This exercise leads to remarkable results. People either see the lost object quite clearly or are led to find it within a very short time.

EXERCISE #2: DISTANT VIEWING

Intuition also involves perceiving the world in a way that is impossible when the five senses limit you. To give you confidence that you have this kind of perception:

1. Find a partner with whom to perform the following exercise.
2. As you sit quietly in one room, have your partner go into the next room where you have placed a stack of picture books or magazines.
3. Tell your partner to open one at random and stare for a moment at any picture.
4. As your partner views the image, see it in your own mind.
5. Don't strain; let any image flash across your mind that wants to.
6. Whether the image is perfectly clear or not, describe what you saw to your partner, once you are both back in the same room.

The secret to success here is not to interpret. Images from the intuitive domain are usually faint at first, so you will get vague hints of the picture—a mountain may seem like just a curved line against the sky or a pointed shape like a witch's hat. Perhaps only a color will come through. Your mind may interpret these vague indicators and come up with the wrong image. Yet be certain that there is a real signal being sent and received.

Repeat the exercise three or four times. Switch with your partner and become the sender instead of the receiver. If you work in a relaxed frame of mind and know that the picture can be seen, you will surprise yourself by your growing accuracy.

EXERCISE #3: "ASK AND YOU SHALL RECEIVE"

Intuition brings answers that are not usually available to us. When you have done your best to solve a problem and yet the solution just won't present itself, you are not defeated—you are ready for a breakthrough. A breakthrough is a jump from reason to intuition, whether it be through dreams, flashes of insight, or suddenly knowing the truth. There is a law of consciousness at work here: "Ask and you shall receive."

Take a problem or challenge currently facing you that has not yet been solved. It can be anything at work or in your private life. Before going to bed tonight, do the following things:

1. Find a time when you are alert and not fatigued. Sit with your eyes closed and quiet your mind by stopping its internal dialogue.
2. State the problem to yourself as clearly as you can.
3. Tell yourself what you expect to happen. Now consciously give your expectations back to the universe. Be open to whatever needs to happen, not what you expect.
4. Ask yourself if you have gathered enough information to solve the problem. If other people are involved, have you gotten their input? If the

situation has several external factors, do you understand them fully? If you don't, gather more information before you proceed further.

5. As you ask for an answer to the problem, give it back to the universe—detach yourself from the outcome.

6. Be willing to receive the answer from any direction. Surrender any attachment to a specific outcome.

7. When you go to bed, expect the answer to be given to you while you sleep.

8. When you wake up the next morning, do not get out of bed. Keeping your eyes closed, search inside for your answer. Listen quietly to whatever comes to you. Sweep away confused or partial images. Wait for an answer that is clear, simple, definite, and satisfying. When you have your answer, act on it.

9. If your solution hasn't arrived, be patient. Go about your daily affairs. Intuition doesn't always have same-day delivery. Be ready for a flash of insight at the most unexpected moments.

At first, this exercise may feel foreign, but it has remarkable power if you practice it enough. The principle of "ask and you shall receive" draws upon awareness at its deepest and clearest level. It has led to many discoveries and insights, all based on trusting one's intuition and nurturing it. By trusting in a higher intelligence (which does not have to be a religious concept—you can equally trust in a higher self or cosmic mind), you open the way for communicating with it. Ultimately, the mystery of intuition isn't a mystery at all. It is the normal process of communicating with the higher intelligence present behind every situation.

CHAKRA 5

Magical Words

FIFTH CHAKRA

Location: *Throat*

Theme: *Speech, self-expression*

Desirable qualities:

Speaking the truth without fear

Authenticity

Eloquence

Language is a component of abundance that is often overlooked. Success in school from first grade onward is correlated with verbal ability. Relationships succeed or falter depending on how well two people communicate. You earn or lose other people's respect according to their trust in what you say. In short, the words you use have immense power.

What people miss is the magic behind language. Words are magical, and how you use their magical properties determines how your life is going to unfold. Every word you speak presents a mystery. How do chemical reactions and electrical charges in brain cells turn into the words we hear in our heads? The brain is using the same basic elements as skin or liver cells, yet the components of these cells neither think nor speak. In everyday life, these mysteries go unsolved; nobody even brings them up.

The fifth chakra, located in the throat, gives you the key to the magic of language by seeing words as expressions, not of brain cells, but of creative intelligence. Here bliss-consciousness transforms itself into all forms of expression but especially speech. (Humans don't even need to speak words. We have body language and facial expressions. According to the experts, we use our hands in over two hundred gestures, each with its own meaning. You'll win a smile by holding up a thumb, but not by holding up a middle finger.)

Your words either help you to achieve the life you want or keep you from it. This sounds stark, but it is inescapable. An attitude of abundance, while important, isn't enough. Thoughts, words, and actions must unfold along a path to fulfillment. In the Middle Way of Buddhism, this path is marked by right thought, right speech, and right action.

The fifth chakra is concerned with right speech, but what does *right* actually mean? Several things are involved:

- Speaking the truth

- Not resisting and opposing

- Supporting your own life and the life of others

- Contributing to peace; avoiding violence

- Being aligned with your dharma

If you had to think through this list every time you opened your mouth, you'd barely say a word. But the chakra system simplifies matters by saying that words are right when they maintain the quality of bliss-consciousness. "Follow your bliss" holds true at every chakra, especially here. With this inner guide, you can promote the good magic in words and avoid the bad magic.

GOOD MAGIC OR BAD?

When you speak a word, you either support the flow of creative intelligence or you block it. Words have the magic to change any situation, either in the right or wrong direction. "I love you" has transformed countless lives in the right direction. "No" has pushed countless situations in the wrong direction.

There are no cut-and-dried rules, however. Always saying yes can work out as badly as always saying no. You have to be aware of how the specific situation is going and what is required. Fortunately, this isn't as mysterious as it sounds. The flow of creative intelligence supports good magic. Your words will be aligned with the best outcome in any situation. Bad magic is the opposite. It isn't bad in the sense of being evil or morally wrong. *Bad* means that you have deviated from the path creative intelligence wants to take.

There are simple, easily recognized signals to show you how a situation is unfolding.

GOOD MAGIC IS AT WORK WHEN

The atmosphere is relaxed.

The other person (or persons) shows good body language.

Your words are greeted with smiles, nods, and other signs of agreement.

You are enjoying what you say.

Issues are being cleared up.

You feel that you are speaking your truth.

There is a sense of peace in the room.

Creative answers are emerging.

Everyone shows signs of cooperating.

You feel heard and understood.

None of these signals are difficult to spot, but often we don't give them enough importance. Instead, we plow ahead, even in the absence of good magic. Consider how often you've found yourself in conversations or meetings where you sense, sometimes, too late, that things have gotten off track. The signals of this are also quite easy to spot.

BAD MAGIC IS AT WORK WHEN

The atmosphere is tense.

The other person (or persons) shows tight body language.

Your words are greeted with blank stares or boredom.
You are not enjoying what you say.
Issues are getting confused and more tangled up.
You feel that your words are ineffectual.
There is a sense of conflict or opposition in
the room.
No consensus is emerging on how to move forward.
You don't feel heard or understood.

Being aware of how different good magic feels from bad magic is an important step. You are getting a clear sense of how right speech is meant to work. The next step is to bring creative intelligence to your aid. You don't have to try to manipulate a bad situation to turn it in the right direction. Aligning yourself with creative intelligence prevents the bad situation from happening. As we will see, this is the most natural way to have your words lead to success and fulfillment.

WHERE THE MAGIC COMES FROM

If a word meant only its dictionary definition, there would be no magic. But words carry other meanings hidden from view. Consider the following example of two people having a quick verbal exchange:

Person A: *Have you seen where I left my car keys?*
Person B: *No.*

On paper, this is a basic exchange of information with no special undertones. In real life, however, the message is very different, filled with implications hidden beneath and behind every word. Let's say that Person A is a wife who happens to be late heading out to work, and Person B is her unemployed husband. She asks, "Have you seen my keys?" without any implication beyond a set of misplaced keys.

But what about his "No"? An unemployed husband could be feeling resentment, depression, self-pity, envy, or victimization, knowing that his wife has a job and he doesn't. Depending on those feelings, "No" could be an emotional response. As outsiders reading this brief exchange on paper (or on-screen), we don't know how their relationship is going. Maybe the man enjoys being a stay-at-home husband. His "No" might just be a simple no.

What does this demonstrate? In every word we speak, there are layers of communication. This is where the magic comes in, because in some mysterious way humans are able to send and receive all kinds of invisible signals contained in no dictionary. We don't often think that words have this much power, but the next sentence you speak will say a lot about the following:

- Your mood.

- Your relationship to the other person.

- Your role in the situation.

- Your state of dominance or submission.

- What you understand.

- What you have to express.

- How much you are willing to cooperate.

- How much emotion you are investing or withholding.

Every word is like the tip of an iceberg, with the major part of the iceberg out of sight. Yet, even at this level, there is communication. We convey so much beneath the surface that other people know—or *think they know*—who we are.

The throat chakra is the place from which you say what you want to say without fear. I remember decades ago when I was nervously preparing to give my first public speech. I felt anxious, even though in medical school and during my internship I confidently spoke up about the things a doctor has to speak about, namely, the diagnosis of what the patient was suffering from, the recommended treatment, and the patient's prognosis for recovery.

Although many people become very anxious if asked to speak in public, I wasn't afraid, exactly; in fact, I was eager to give my talk. But I wasn't sure how the audience would respond to me. It was the early eighties. I was taking my first steps into meditation and the mind-body connection, two things that mainstream doctors and much of the public felt skepticism or outright hostility toward.

At this point a friend, who happened to be a meditation teacher, gave me a piece of invaluable advice: "People aren't going to respond by what you say. They are going to respond by who you are." In other words, if I speak the most beautiful and affective words, but I am closed off, fearful, and uncertain, my message will fall flat.

This is the ultimate magic of words—we can animate them. Words are energized by what we carry within us. Words are just letters and sounds, but we have the power to breathe life into them. Too often, however, we strip the magic from our words by speaking out of fear, self-doubt, and the need to disguise the truth from ourselves and others. When this happens, right speech collapses into wrong speech.

MAGICAL LIES

Part of the ego's agenda is to present a strong self-image to the world. But this effort keeps you disconnected from your true self. If you lived from the level of your true self, you wouldn't need any image at all. This is the quality known as authenticity. Children are authentic in an innocent, open way, but very quickly they learn that parental judgment is at work. Being told that you are "good" or "bad" is life-changing if these words come from a parent and are repeated often enough.

To be a good boy or girl becomes every child's motivation. The chances of failure are dire. "Bad" children may be marked for life psychologically. But their fate isn't fixed. A bad child can decide at a certain age that his parents were wrong—or need to be proved wrong—which can lead in a positive direction. Yet the opposite is more often the case. Bad children become discouraged, and there is much less chance that they will ever believe "I am enough."

There is a huge gray area between such stark labels as *good* and *bad*. Inside this area we create our self-image, driven by the insecurity of the ego. Most people harbor a host of fictions that they project through their self-image. I call these fictions "magical lies." They reflect the ego's ability to fool us, the people we relate to, and the world at large. As a result, we are driven by hidden beliefs that have no basis in the ever-flowing true self.

Pause for a moment and consider which of the ego's magical lies might be influencing you right now.

A Web of Magical Lies

- I am alone and separate from other people.

- I was born one day.

- I will die one day.

- External forces buffet me around, beyond my control.

- My life is barely a speck in the vast cosmos.

- I am engaged in a personal struggle.

- I seek to maximize pleasure and minimize pain.

- I am influenced by past memories, traumas, and setbacks.

- I fear failure.

- I am trapped in this aging body.

- I have inner conflicts.

- I am not sure I am lovable.

- I am prone to anxiety and depression.

- I live in a dangerous world.

- I need to be careful about many things.

- I take care of myself, knowing that no one else will.

- I am not enough.

You don't have to say these things out loud. Human speech is filled with hints and implications. We are constantly drawing inferences that the speaker might want to hide but which, reading between the lines, reflect the amazing fact that words reveal layers of meaning. The last line on the list of the ego's magical lies, "I am not enough," is the greatest lie and also the most powerful. It is taking a whole book to undo it.

No matter how different any two people are, everyone is engaged in the same project: creating a story about themselves. In almost everyone's life, the result is a confused jumble, where past experience and future hopes are mashed up with whatever is happening today. In this confusion, too many people do not get what they want from their story.

For example, suppose it's Saturday, and you've just come to the breakfast table. Like many people, you feel a little groggy before you've poured your first cup of coffee. Your spouse or partner asks, "How did you sleep?" With your next word you will cross a threshold: Your story for that day is about to go public. You are sharing your thoughts with another person, and for the rest of the day your words belong to everyone you interact with.

Suppose you aren't interested in sharing just then, so when your partner asks how you slept, you mutter "Fine" in a flat voice and turn away. Freeze frame. In a single gesture lasting only a few seconds, you've done something magical, and it probably happened totally unconsciously. You channeled infinite possibilities into the real world. Using what the English writer Aldous Huxley called "the reducing valve," you turned thousands of possible replies into just one terse word.

Don't be too quick to unfreeze the frame, because if you shrug this example off as mundane and insignificant, you are throwing away the magical aspect. At the instant you reduce thousands of possible words into just one—"Fine"—you have used a speck of creative intelligence. But it isn't really a speck. Your story is like a mental hologram, in which the whole image is revealed by a single detail.

The ability to make mental holograms is innate, inherited at birth, and universal. You use it every day, taking a single scrap of experience and blowing it up into a picture or, rather, a movie. The face of someone you love isn't just a set of features—your whole relationship is compressed inside this one visual image. If you play the piano, touching the keys brings up all your skill, training, and musical tastes. To a physicist reading a set of symbols, $E = mc^2$ unfolds the revolution brought about by Einstein's General Theory of Relativity.

The upshot is that your story is too vast to be controlled by your mind or ego. Only creative intelligence foresees where your story is going, what it really means, and which direction in the plot is the right one for you to take. Right speech isn't about the words you choose to say. It is about where the words come from.

UPGRADING YOUR STORY

There are too many words in your story—past, present, and future—to mentally assess, but your story is constantly projecting the hologram of you. Or, to be more accurate, the "you" that conforms to "I am enough" or "I am not enough." One or the other pervades your story. "I am not enough" is projected by the following:

- Complaining
- Blaming other people
- Shirking responsibility
- Being uncommunicative
- Acting like a petty tyrant or perfectionist
- Making someone else look small so that you look larger
- Being defensive
- Never revealing weakness or vulnerability
- Acting emotionally uptight
- Offering little or no praise to others
- Pessimism
- Fear of intimacy
- Blind adherence to rules

In their own way, each of these behaviors is a disguise for self-judgment. The first step in upgrading your story is to begin to notice any time you exhibit these behaviors. The list is long, so jot down in a notebook just a single behavior that you think might apply to you. Be on the lookout for this behavior—perhaps it is complaining or blaming others—and put a check in your notebook page.

Do this for a week, and then take stock of your tendency to complain or blame others. The next step is to stop yourself whenever you catch yourself behaving this way. Simply stopping, though difficult at first, is very effective. If you have time, you can then get to a quiet place where you can center yourself and be in simple awareness. Harried parents, for instance, can find respite by spending some time in the family bathroom.

Because karma forms in repeated patterns, you will tend to find that the behavior that reflects "I am not enough" in your situation is well known to the people around you. Your primary goal is to diminish and then eliminate only the most prominent reflections. When you feel secure enough, sit down with a close friend or confidant (not your partner or spouse, because this relationship is too emotionally charged), and ask which behaviors are the most obvious in yourself. You are seeking a sympathetic, helpful answer, not criticism. You'll be surprised at the things other people see very easily in you that you might be totally blind to. Welcome this input because, by becoming more aware, you can begin to change.

There is also the other side of the coin to consider. When there is little or no self-judgment, "I am enough" is projected by the following:

- Emotional openness and honesty
- Sympathy for others
- Giving and being of service
- Tolerance of mistakes—yours and other people's

- Easy acceptance of other people
- Tolerance of different attitudes and beliefs
- Optimism
- A willingness to freely share credit
- Not criticizing anyone in front of other people
- Generous appreciation of other people
- Welcoming intimacy in relationships
- Being able to love and be loved

It's a pleasure to upgrade your story by strengthening these qualities. Note which ones you most value, and begin to notice situations where you can express them. This side of you is also karmic, because it fits into a repeated pattern. Such patterns become unconscious and automatic. In that light, you might seek out a confidant and ask which of these behaviors you might not be exhibiting. Perhaps you have no difficulty sharing credit, in which case this isn't an area to focus on. But you might be uneasy accepting people who are too different from you. Then this is the area to focus on. Don't force yourself to change. Just have the intention and look for situations where you can comfortably show acceptance and appreciation.

Using both of these strategies—undoing the negative side and doing more on the positive side—you are steadily forging an open line of communication with your true self. It knows what you intend, and you will witness that upgrading your story becomes easier and more joyful as you go along.

TALKING ABOUT RELATIONSHIPS

It has become a cliché to say that a healthy relationship depends on good communication, but if you pause for a moment, words are the most constant ingredient in your relationship. The words "I love you" are wonderful to hear, but they occupy the tiniest sliver of the words you and your partner will exchange. In marriage counseling, the most common complaint is "He [or she] doesn't listen." Of course this is not true in the literal sense. Unless you are skilled at shutting other people out—a skill too easily developed in a long-term relationship, sadly—you are constantly listening.

What actually matters is being heard. When you are heard, you are valued. The words themselves are secondary and often irrelevant. People want to know that they matter; they want to reassure themselves that the bond with their partner is still strong; they look for validation in the other person's eyes. If you trust that you are being heard, the way is open to revealing yourself more and more. Then the relationship begins to work at the level of the true self. When someone yearns for a spiritual relationship, this bond at the level of the true self is the key.

When a relationship begins to unravel, one or both partners say, "We've grown too far apart." Sometimes the statement is bitter, sometimes not. But in either case, growing apart means that the bond from self to self has been frayed or torn apart. From the ego level, the trouble is that "I"—including my way of doing things, my attitudes, my goals in life—have been ignored. An ego agenda has gone off the rails, and the partner who is dissatisfied needs a new ally to carry out what "I" want.

I'd like to address relationships where two people want things to work out well and desire a lasting bond of love. The ideal way to achieve this is to realize the part played by consciousness. Creative intelligence doesn't flow just through individuals. It flows just as much through relationships.

Words play a key role here. At any moment you can take up the thread of creative intelligence. First, be aware of when the thread is lost or broken. You are losing the thread whenever your words:

Incite division and opposition.

Express hostility.

Increase anxiety in yourself and your partner.

Fuel the ongoing drama.

Complain about your partner's behavior.

Shift responsibility and blame to your partner.

Put other people down.

Shut someone else out.

Try to dominate and control.

Puff up your self-importance.

These things are obvious results of the words you speak, and they cannot be mistaken as positive and life-supporting. I'm using the word "partner" in this section, but everything applies equally well to being a parent or friend. You have to be alert enough to catch yourself breaking the thread. We are quick enough to spot faults in others, but very slow in seeing that what we most dislike about someone else is precisely what we deny about ourselves. If we deny that we are doing what we condemn in other people, our self-denial falls under the label of a magical lie. Denial and egotism keep the lie alive.

No one is totally immersed in the false beliefs, denial, and ego-driven speech I've just listed. Creative intelligence surfaces sometimes, and then your words nurture your relationship. You are aligned with creative intelligence whenever your words

Express love, gratitude, and appreciation.

Connect you to your partner.

Tell the truth without hurting.

Show sympathy.

Add to the solution of a problem.

Create a positive atmosphere.

Offer hope and help.

Celebrate the gifts you have been given.

None of these things require you to be superhuman or saintly. A loving parent would naturally use words this way in raising a child. Somewhere along the way, many people have taught themselves to block the flow of creative intelligence. Unfortunately, this has been injurious to everyone's relationship. Yet Yoga teaches that bliss-consciousness stands firm, no matter how far we stray into self-defeating or destructive behavior. The generosity of spirit cannot be thwarted.

Your words reveal who you are at a level of awareness that fits the ego agenda. The same goes for your partner. But in a loving relationship, this isn't the basis of your bond. Instead, you are obeying the magnetic attraction that one true self has for another. When you see that this is true, you know why your relationship exists, not for ego-driven reasons but as an expression of bliss-consciousness. It isn't necessary for you to convince your partner of this. Your own knowledge is enough. It connects you to the generosity of spirit, and that will be enough. If you and your partner is on the same wavelength, nothing is more beautiful than two people evolving together. The best way to reach that state is to evolve within yourself. Then you become the embodiment of the generosity of spirit.

It is disturbing, particularly for people who place a high value on their spiritual growth, to feel that the other person is pulling away. A rift is opened, and the relationship begins to feel more and more unequal. You are trying to follow your higher guidance, but your partner has other things in mind, other pursuits and values. In due course, once the rift is too wide, the relationship might be seriously coming apart. What started out with high hopes of a spiritual connection binding two loving partners could well end in the same ugly recriminations and disappointment that occur in any broken relationship.

Yoga's message might be hard to hear, but the behavior of your partner reflects where you are. In the state of detachment, this knowledge enables you to stop casting blame and to focus on your own state of awareness. Detachment is a healing state, not an isolated, lonely one that needs the other person to be good in every way you desire. In subtle ways the ego agenda undermines detachment, making it "my" spiritual ideals versus "your" failings. The inner work is always personal, intimate, and invisible. Yet it is the greatest work you can do in your relationship.

Life is infinitely capable of supporting itself. When you detach from your ego, you side with life in all its wholeness. Your trust grows, step by step, until the ultimate mystery is revealed: Life and bliss are one and the same. Lack and want have never had the truth on their side.

ACTIVATING THE THROAT CHAKRA

This chakra strengthens every aspect of speech and self-expression. A few things you can do apply to every chakra in general:

- Be in simple awareness. When you notice that you aren't, take a few minutes to center yourself.
- Meditate on the mantra *Ham* (page 84).
- Meditate on the centering thought "I am free expression" or "I speak my truth" (page 87).

Other steps are more specifically aimed at activating the throat chakra. You are constantly projecting your story, and Yoga teaches that improving your story happens in consciousness. Much depends on activating the fifth chakra so that you are speaking the truth of "I am enough." You can do this by consciously changing the story line you are telling, not to others, but to yourself.

Exercise: Take five or ten minutes to be alone in the morning. Sit with your eyes closed and see yourself facing the challenge in the day ahead. Pick something current, a situation that seems stuck or not working out the way you want it to.

In your mind's eye visualize a stumbling block—this could be a person, an upcoming meeting, a point of resistance, a lack of communication. Most of us have no trouble envisioning bad scenarios and anticipated threats. That's the viewpoint of "I am not enough."

See the situation as if you were watching a movie and being allowed to direct it. Let the movie unfold, and when you get to a bad part, run it backwards. If someone has come into the room to put up obstacles or complain, watch the person back out in reverse and come in again. You are freeing up a tense expectation and gaining control over it.

Repeat this exercise until you no longer feel tense and frustrated. Having control over your visualization is a powerful way to allow creative intelligence to flow, and nothing is more important. You are a co-creator in every situation you find yourself in. You want to regain the creative role. Otherwise, the situation is controlling you.

The same exercise works for enhancing a relationship or any situation that is working out well. Think of an upcoming moment in the day, and see it as a movie. In the movie, visualize your partner acting perfectly or the situation being resolved in total harmony. Run the scene backwards, and replay it. Repeat until you feel fulfilled and confident about your new vision.

Don't expect instant results or the best outcome every time. But the process will evolve as long as you step aside and let creative intelligence take over. It gets its cue from your inner vision of the best outcome. That is enough to improve your story from the level of consciousness, which is the most powerful level for change in an evolutionary direction.

CHAKRA 4

Heartfelt Emotions

FOURTH CHAKRA

Location: Heart

Theme: Emotions

Desirable qualities:

    Happiness

    Love

    Emotional intelligence

    Empathy, bonding

Humans are the only living creatures who have trouble being happy. If the chakra system can solve this problem, it will make a huge contribution to a person's life. Happiness is an emotional state, and emotions are symbolically centered in the fourth chakra, which is located at the heart. In its state of abundant natural balance, the heart chakra is the source of happiness, but also emotional expression of every sort. That's already our common understanding when we talk about having a happy heart or a sad heart, a full heart or an empty heart. The ancient Indian yogis agreed. They went so far as to talk about the wisdom of the heart, because with each chakra a new mode of knowing emerges. It is just as wise, and perhaps wiser, to *feel* your way through life as it is to *think* your way through life.

In the fourth chakra, creative intelligence undergoes a transformation into emotions. Because we are still talking about bliss-consciousness, which is the source of all transformations, emotions are meant to be life-enhancing as feelings of love and joy but also compassion, empathy, intimacy, forgiveness, hope, and optimism. Negative emotions are misaligned. They are untrustworthy guides, even though impulses of anger, fear, depression, and jealousy can be powerful. When negative emotions occur, it is an indication that something has gone awry in the flow of creative intelligence. People often feel helpless to change their emotions. But emotions reflect your state of awareness, and in Yoga, when you are in simple awareness, hidden emotional knots get untangled and old karma is diminished; sometimes it completely dissipates. The past, as we'll see, turns out to play an important part in the story.

Part of inner affluence is a rich emotional life, beginning with your right to be happy. But modern psychology has found it nearly impossible to decide for certain if humans are even meant to be happy. Psychotherapy has a poor success rate at curing depression and anxiety, the chief obstacles to feeling happy, which is why the vast majority of patients are sent away with prescriptions for antidepressants and tranquilizers. These drugs lessen the symptoms of anxiety and depression without offering a cure, and they are often unreliable even in achieving symptom relief.

Yoga isn't a branch of medicine or psychotherapy, but it offers deeper knowledge about how consciousness works, which lies at the heart of emotions, since they are transformations of consciousness. If your emotional life is troubled, conflicted, or unsatisfactory, you inevitably become emotionally diminished. Taken to an extreme, a person can exist in a state of emotional poverty. This is something we each have to take responsibility for, because the emotional choices we make are not predestined.

I am not discounting family upbringing. Every child is deeply influenced by love or the lack of it, and there are cases—unfortunately, far too many—where mistreatment and abuse create long-lasting pain and distress. But the healing process isn't accomplished by erasing the past, blaming your family, or depending on someone else to change you. The healing process occurs inside you, which makes you both healer and healed.

Self-awareness is the starting point, so pause and consider how much you are affected by emotional poverty:

Symptoms of Emotional Poverty

- Feeling worried and anxious

- Having a short temper

- Finding it hard to express love and affection

- Being afraid of intimacy

- Feeling embarrassed to show your emotions

- Feeling embarrassed when someone else shows their emotions

- Believing that a show of emotions is a sign of weakness

- Believing that "real men don't cry"

- Judging women for being "too emotional"

- Finding it hard to express how you really feel

- Hiding from your true feelings

- Harboring secret emotional trauma or abuse in your past

- Holding on to grudges

- Finding it difficult to forgive

- Being haunted by past humiliations and failures

- Seeing yourself as a loser

- Stubbornly holding on to feelings of anger, jealousy, resentment, and revenge

- Feeling sad for no reason

- Feeling helpless and hopeless

I think most people will be shocked at how long this list is. It is just as shocking to realize how many symptoms of emotional poverty are all around us—and inside us. Freud invented a term—"the psychopathology of every life"—to indicate how common psychological distress actually is. We are fooling ourselves when we pigeonhole the people we consider crazy, maladjusted, peculiar, neurotic, troubled, and therefore psychologically abnormal. Everyone's daily life has a psychological undercurrent. No one escapes at least a few symptoms of emotional poverty, which appear long before a person needs help from a therapist.

You can understand why most people are very reluctant to explore their emotions in any depth. When we experience psychological pain, most of us practice some form of avoidance. We keep quiet about our distress, trying to hide it from others out of shame. We go into denial or seek distraction by watching TV, playing video games, drinking alcohol, and so forth—any temporary relief from emotional pain feels less threatening than actually addressing the problem.

Healing begins—without shame, panic, fear, and trepidation—when you accept that a state of inner fulfillment is accessible. In its balanced state, the heart chakra overflows with happiness; it takes time and effort to spoil this state. Our task is to undo all that misspent time and effort. No one should be experiencing emotional poverty. A rich emotional life, which you have a right to lead, has the following qualities:

Symptoms of Emotional Richness

- You are in touch with your emotions.

- You pay attention to how you feel.

- You trust your emotional responses and are guided by them.

- Fear and worry are not in control of your life.

- You bounce back from negative emotions.

- You don't cling to anger, jealousy, and resentment.

- You enjoy intimacy with the one you love.

- You can express love and affection freely.

- You are not embarrassed to show your feelings.

- You are not burdened by past humiliation and failure.

- You are generous about expressing your feelings.

Emotional healing is intimate, and it works best if you are easy with yourself. In a gentle metaphor, the Vedic tradition in India refers to the healing process as "blowing dust off a mirror." The dust is the accumulation of memories and old experiences that give rise to inner suffering. The mirror is simple awareness, reflecting only bliss-consciousness in all its guises.

HOW EMOTIONS EVOLVE

Many people distrust their emotions and hide from them; other people magnify their emotions and use them to manipulate a situation and get what they want. Because of this, you might well be reluctant to go on a journey that takes you through the dark forest of suppressed, toxic emotions. Two reassurances need to be offered. First, there is no need to explore the dark forest of the unconscious. Emotional healing occurs by allowing bliss-consciousness to restore itself. From the perspective of simple awareness, the whole mind is conscious. We hide from our emotions at the level of the ego. Creative intelligence operates at a deeper level. Secondly, an emotional journey is nothing to fear or avoid; you are already on that journey and have been since birth. Your emotions are part of everything you say, think, and do.

It would be nice if the only task ahead were to reclaim the inner child, which has become a kind of emotional ideal of innocence. But a child's emotional life is immature and unevolved. The basics are there, waiting to be shaped, ranging from pure joy to powerful anger and fear. If you do not evolve beyond the basics, however, you carry into later life the destructive side of the inner child. The inner child doesn't vanish in adults, and sometimes it still exerts great power. Everything depends on whether or not the infantile part of you is contributing to your emotional well-being.

HOW IS YOUR INNER CHILD?

We learn life lessons in childhood, and this applies to our emotions. To give yourself an idea of how well your past is treating you today, answer the following questions by checking *Yes* or *No*. Be as honest with yourself as you can without going too easy or being too self-critical.

I am generally even-tempered.
    Yes ☐   No ☐

I am not prone to sudden outbursts.
    Yes ☐   No ☐

I don't react impulsively.
    Yes ☐   No ☐

I can take criticism pretty well.
    Yes ☐   No ☐

I find it easy to be happy for someone else's good fortune.
    Yes ☐   No ☐

I don't hold grudges.
    Yes ☐   No ☐

I don't indulge in revenge fantasies.
    Yes ☐   No ☐

I can remember recent moments of joy.
    Yes ☐   No ☐

The happiness of others is important to me.
    Yes ☐   No ☐

I consider rivals to be competitors, not enemies.
Yes ☐   No ☐

I can listen patiently to someone else's woes.
Yes ☐   No ☐

My emotions don't get me into trouble, such as heated
arguments.
Yes ☐   No ☐

I am comfortable being warm and affectionate.
Yes ☐   No ☐

I value being loved and lovable.
Yes ☐   No ☐

My parents were good examples of emotional maturity.
Yes ☐   No ☐

I don't immediately strike back if someone gets angry
with me.
Yes ☐   No ☐

I don't care too much if I am liked or disliked.
Yes ☐   No ☐

I find most people likable.
Yes ☐   No ☐

I tend to see the best in others rather than the worst.
Yes ☐   No ☐

I am accepting. I am not quick to criticize others.
Yes ☐   No ☐

I can usually tell what someone else is feeling even
when they try to hide it.
Yes ☐   No ☐

I feel compassion for those in trouble.

Yes ☐   No ☐

I laugh easily.

Yes ☐   No ☐

I enjoy the company of children.

Yes ☐   No ☐

I know what it feels like to be spiritually uplifted.

Yes ☐   No ☐

Total Yes _____·   Total No _____

ASSESSING YOUR SCORE

If your inner child is perfectly happy and balanced, you will score Yes twenty-five times, and if your inner child is suffering and out of balance, you will score No twenty-five times. Nobody can achieve such an absolute score either way, because everyone's inner life is mixed. What you need to notice is the ratio of Yes to No answers. The more Yes answers you have, the better.

18–24 YES: You have evolved very well emotionally and have helped your inner child grow in understanding and acceptance. You demonstrate a good combination of feeling secure in your emotional life and also responding well to the emotions of others. You don't crave approval or cringe from disapproval. Your emotional reactions are considered, tempered by experience, reason, and maturity.

13–17 YES: Your emotional life falls somewhere in the middle, close to the social norm. Your inner child is insecure at times. You probably don't value your emotions or trust them entirely. Instead, you find yourself ambushed by unwanted emotions that you'd much rather avoid. If you are introverted, you keep your feelings to yourself. If you are extroverted, your emotions are out there for all the world to see. You are likely to be fond of escaping into romantic fantasies, either in imagination or through movies and books.

1–12 YES: Your inner child has a negative influence over you, and the lower your score, the more self-defeating this influence is. You have a hard time connecting with mature adults, preferring to be with others who are as immature, pessimistic, self-doubting, and impulsive as you are. At the higher end (10–12 YES), you might notice none of these deficits. Instead, you simply turn your back on emotions, giving great value to being a rational creature on the one hand or highly self-disciplined on the other. In any case, you judge against people who show their emotions easily. You might feel superior to them. Tending to your own life with its ups and downs, you have little sympathy for people who don't just get on with it and solve their own problems. In your view, the more emotional you are, the weaker you seem to others and yourself.

Let me underscore that most of us find it hard to be completely honest about our emotional lives, so this quiz is just a general guide. It is all too easy for some people to exaggerate their positive qualities as it is for others to exaggerate their faults. Use this quiz simply as a mirror, reflecting back how you feel about your emotions in a general way.

A rich emotional life makes you generous with your feelings, open, and resilient. No child starts out this way, which is why we all need to evolve beyond the emotional life of childhood and adolescence. Yet somewhat paradoxically, there is no agreement over why *Homo sapiens* evolved over millennia to be as emotional as we are.

Evolution hasn't made human nature smooth sailing. Your emotions can provide you with the best and worst moments of your life. Either way, the human mind wants to experience maximum diversity. Just as we never run out of thoughts and words, we never run out of feelings. *Maximum* means what it says—each of us goes far beyond simply wanting consistently nice, pleasant feelings.

Every positive feeling has an opposite that is its shadowy twin, and you can't have one without the other. The tangled web of human emotions is evidenced in phrases like "He's the kind of person you love to hate." Love poetry is filled with the ache of love as well as its delights. Sex was considered the primal pleasure by Freud, but lust is a biblical sin, and Shakespeare communicates the darker emotions surrounding sexual pleasure in Sonnet 129, "Th'expense of spirit in a waste of shame / Is lust in action." Yet matters of the heart, in general, are nakedly exposed to the shadow.

Rather amazingly, it is impossible to explain why humans have emotions in the first place. Other creatures exhibit impulses that tempt us to equate them with our own feelings. After an elephant dies, the rest of the herd will stand around the body quietly for several days, which to human eyes looks like mourning. Dolphins not only wear a permanent smile but seem happy cavorting in the waves. All baby mammals seem to spend much of their time playing, which we'd call having fun. Yet it is impossible for us to know what animals feel. We can't look inside their psyches.

One can connect the most primitive impulses to the lower brain at the base of the skull, where sex drive and fight-or-flight reside. But these are relics from our distant hominid past, if not hundreds of millions of years earlier; it is hard to find a mammal, bird, or reptile that doesn't exhibit the same drives. What held every creature in good stead somehow wasn't good enough for *Homo sapiens*. We are the only creatures that distrust our basic impulses. Has evolution done this to us over the course of millennia?

I believe that our emotions work against Darwinian survival. For example, we humans take care of the old, the sick, and the disabled. This is a form of artificial survival, since natural selection weeds out the weak, the sick, and the old. (Nor can we point to compassion having roots in higher primates in the forest. Alpha males dominate the weak out of total selfishness, using ferocity and violence.)

The purpose of emotions is revealed not in Darwinian terms but at the level of consciousness. An ancient Indian spiritual text on love, the *Brihadaranyaka Upanishad*, has it right. The text takes the form of a queen wanting to hear the most secret wisdom of her husband, the king, and their dialogue is intimate, simple, and honest. In the most important line of the *Upanishad*, the king declares, "All love is for the sake of the Self."

It might seem, wrongly, that the king is saying "All love is selfish." What he actually means is this: We seem to love another person for their body or mind, but in reality all love comes from a deeper source. One can call this source the soul or the Self. The capital *S* is used to designate that this Self is beyond the ego. In other words, the Self is each person's portion of pure awareness, the soul. To love someone else forms an emotional bond from Self to Self, from consciousness to consciousness, from soul to soul.

EVOLVING EMOTIONALLY

All along, I've said that you can trust creative intelligence to give you everything you need for what you need to do. This holds true for your emotions. There are emotions you need to lead a successful, fulfilled life, and emotions you do not need.

Few of us approach emotions in this way. Instead, we put labels on positive emotions and negative emotions, which is useful as far as it goes. But look at anger, which is sometimes negative, sometimes positive, and sometimes totally toxic. Can you live without anger, banishing all forms of it from your emotional makeup? One of the virtues that an enlightened person arrives at, according to Yoga, is *Ahimsa*, which is usually translated as "nonviolent" or "doing no harm." But this isn't the same as banishing anger, because anger isn't the same as violence.

Strange as it might sound, there is loving anger and peaceful anger. A mother can scold a toddler for writing on the walls with crayon without losing her love for her child. You can express anger over crime and war, while still remaining peaceful at heart. What matters is your intention. If you use anger with a negative intent, this transforms anger into something dark and threatening. We all sense this. We know when someone is just angry and when someone takes anger a step further by attacking us or trying to dominate. I knew a woman who in late life converted to Buddhism, and one reason for doing so was her guilt over having been such an angry, forceful, domineering mother.

When her children were young, she got as angry as she pleased whenever she pleased. One might call this selfish or narcissistic anger. Afterwards, once she calmed down, she didn't apologize, either. Somehow, she ignored the destructive rupture that was developing with her children. She talked to me about her sorrow that her two sons, now all grown up, couldn't accept her as a peaceful Buddhist.

"I don't get angry with them anymore," she said, "and I bend over backwards to show them how much I love them. But around me they act stiff and distant. What can I do?"

"Make peace with how things are, and let them change in their own good time," I said, not very confidently.

"But it's been years now," she wailed.

It won't surprise you to know what had gone wrong. Her sons were imprinted by their mother's anger, not because she lost her temper—all parents do—but because of the intention behind her anger. This intention said, "You don't count." Of course, she didn't verbalize this message, but it was received anyway, using a child's emotional antennas, which are very sensitive. It takes time to harden our hearts as we grow up, but that's what had happened here. As young boys, her sons had hardened their hearts against their mother in order to defend themselves from the next time she sent a blast of rage their way.

Carrying the burden of past hurts and wounds inside you causes a condition known as "emotional debt" (the term was popularized by the late psychiatrist David Viscott in his writings). What causes emotional debt? Not the emotions of anger, anxiety, envy, jealousy, or anything else. By themselves, these emotions can't do lasting harm until they are attached to intentions. Together, a bad intention coupled with a negative emotion creates the emotional debt everyone has accumulated from the past.

WHERE EMOTIONAL DEBT COMES FROM

The past is woven into our emotional makeup. Old hurts and wounds have made an impression, the same way your thumb makes an impression on soft clay. However, emotional wounds do this invisibly. When you feel anger, anxiety, jealousy, or another emotion you later regret, your past is speaking to you. When you vent anger or express worry to another person, your past is speaking through you.

To pay off your emotional debt once and for all, you first need to know where it came from. As you read the following list, pause and refer each item back to yourself, seeing if you can identify any occasion when you were the target. Typically, these incidents occur in the family.

Emotional debt occurs when:

Someone directs violence at you. This violence can
    be physical or mental, a burst of rage or a slap in
    the face.
You were bullied at school or made to feel stupid by a
    teacher.
You were punished unfairly, and pleas of innocence did
    no good.
Someone hurts your feelings and doesn't care. The
    hidden message is that you don't count.
A person seems to like you but then commits a casual
    act of betrayal, such as gossiping behind your back
    or sharing a secret they promised not to reveal.
A person withholds love to manipulate you. The hidden
    message is, "If you love me, I can get you to do what
    I want."
An intimate partner betrays you sexually with some-
    one else.
Competition goes beyond rivalry or a game and
    becomes more like war. In such situations, you
    are blindsided by the attack, which exposes your

vulnerability. The message is, "Don't be so trusting. It's a sign of weakness."

A parent shows favoritism for one child over the others. This is most damaging when the child who isn't favored gets blamed and put down to underscore that they aren't worth the same love as the favored child.

A parent shares adult emotions with a young child. The division between child and adult is necessary for a child to feel safe. It creates enormous anxiety if a parent unloads their own worry and anxiety on a child. The result is a kind of emotional knot: The child knows that a parent is in trouble but has no power to improve things.

The list can go on and on, but once you grasp how emotional debt works, you can see the link between a bad intention and the harm it causes. With this awareness, you can start to undo the harm and forgive your emotional debts. We'll go into the healing process next.

FORGIVING YOUR DEBT

The heart chakra is healing when it allows emotional residue from the past to be washed away, not through a painful return to the past but by the abundant flow of creative intelligence. Clearly, you can't have a rich emotional life and still owe emotional debts. The best healer of emotions is emotion itself. Experience a moment of joy and, in that moment, a bit of old sadness dissolves. Like stubborn ink stains on a shirt, it takes more time to wash away stubborn emotional stains, but the method remains the same, and at every stage there is hope and improvement.

To become your own healer, align yourself with creative intelligence, because it wants only what is good for you. At any given moment, your intention is the key. Learn to recognize what your intention really is. Nothing more is needed. You don't have to psychoanalyze yourself or anyone else. Remain centered and be in simple awareness.

Intentions that are aligned with creative intelligence are readily apparent; there is no mystery to them. You have the choice to favor them anytime you want. Intentions are expressed as "I want to" sentences.

The Intentions of Simple Awareness

- I want to be more fulfilled.

- I want to be happier.

- I want peace.

- I want to be creative.

- I want to be a positive influence.

- I want to be open and honest.

- I want what is best for everyone.

- I want what is right and truthful.

- I want to be emotionally close to others.

The flow of creative intelligence supports you in just the ways you need. When you get out of the way, what you need comes about. The problem is that all of us are inconsistent—sometimes we act out of good intentions, but sometimes we don't. Things get complicated, emotions start to work against our happiness, and the situation goes off the rails.

Most people feel ill at ease emotionally, and they react to a strong emotion of anger, fear, or agitation by trying to get rid of it. They do this by passing it along, like throwing a hot potato into someone else's lap. Blame is especially potent, because instead of taking responsibility for your predicament, blaming someone else enables you to absolve yourself and clears away guilt at the same time. Guilt will die down if someone else is to blame. Nothing that goes wrong is your fault.

But passing guilt along constitutes the worst of intentions, because you are doing yourself and other people no good. It isn't hard to recognize when you are playing this emotional con game, which crops up often in relationships. Because a habit like blame is so destructive in relationships, passing it along can be, and should be, abandoned. It's not hard to see how the game is played.

The Tactics of "Pass It Along"

- Attacking

- Blaming

- Clinging

- Dominating

- Manipulating

- Controlling

Each of these requires a little more explanation.

It's important not to gloss over these behaviors and to see where they really come from.

Attacking is anger directed at someone else. We justify this behavior by saying things like "She deserved it" or "I had to defend myself." At the worst of times we don't bother with a justification. Snapping back, showing impatience, putting someone else down, and showing righteous indignation happen unthinkingly. In every case, however, the other person feels attacked. Whatever excuse you come up with, you are the attacker, which is something you must own.

Blaming generally comes directly from the inner child, who doesn't feel adequate or secure enough to handle how it feels. Children turn to their parents whenever they feel overwhelmed; a parent is stronger and more capable. In a distorted way, you are doing the same thing when you blame someone else. You are implicitly acknowledging that you are weak and the other person is stronger. You are asking them to shoulder the burden you can't carry or don't want to. The other person will feel that this is unfair, because blame is unbalanced. You take too little of the burden and pass on too much.

Clinging is also a holdover from childhood. If you look at the behavior of primates, baby monkeys, chimps, lemurs, and all others cling to their mothers and get carried along with them. In this way they feel protected until the world no longer feels threatening, at which point they stop clinging. There is an in-between time when the baby ventures out alone, but at the slightest hint of danger it dashes back to cling to its mother.

In human infants one of the first motor skills is the clinging or grasping with the hand; clinging to the mother when a stranger appears starts as early as nine months. In the case of emotional debt, however, the clinging is emotional. You attach yourself passively to someone you feel is stronger. You let them handle the decision making. In times of stress, you become helpless and need someone else to take care of you. In these situations, the other person feels that they are dealing with a child.

Dominating is a bullying tactic, and although there is a public outcry about the bullying that abounds on social media, which generally targets adolescents and preteens, bullying behavior begins much earlier. If you think like a primatologist who studies the behavior of primates in the wild, bullying is a way of establishing dominance among males in a family or pack (while simultaneously showing females that they are subservient). But the analogy with humans is a poor one. *Homo sapiens*, being self-aware, has no natural need to dominate or give in to others of our kind. We are capable of being self-reliant and self-sufficient. We have the choice to cooperate rather than compete.

Domineering behavior is a regressive shortcut. It is regressive because it reverts to schoolyard bullying and blocks the opportunity for any real emotional back-and-forth or negotiating. A dominant person simply wants the upper hand in every situation. Other people feel that they are being put down and deprived of their right to take credit, share the limelight, and contribute what they have to give.

Manipulating typically grows out of tactics that worked in childhood, when you discover that wheedling and whining get you what you want. You take advantage of a parent's love by selfishly manipulating it. If your inner child has learned that manipulation worked in the past, this tactic carries over into adulthood, taking various forms. You get your way by guilt-tripping the other person for not giving you what you want. You sulk, pout, and withdraw to show how unhappy they have made you. You act histrionically, blowing things out of all proportion. Quite often the targets of this manipulation don't see that they are being manipulated (unless they happen to be expert at it themselves). They begin to notice it when they feel handled or become aware that the other person is faking their reactions out of selfish motives.

Controlling doesn't seem at first glance to grow out of behavior in childhood, but there are crude tactics, like throwing a tantrum in public, that are signs of controlling—as soon as the parent gives in, a two-year-old throwing a tantrum can often turn it off like throwing a switch. But in adults, controlling behavior emerges in more sophisticated ways, such as perfectionism, never being satisfied, or maintaining constant vigilance. A jealous spouse might demand that his partner account for where she is every minute of the day. But just as often there is no obvious motive behind the need to be in control. The roots of controlling behavior may be tangled, yet the other person has no difficulty knowing how it affects them: They feel imprisoned, suffocated, and imposed upon by someone else's will.

ENDING THE GAME

For each of these behaviors I've tried to show how it feels to act a certain way in the game of pass it along but also how it feels when you are the object of the behavior, the one who feels victimized.

If you catch yourself acting out any of these behaviors, stop doing it, pause, and let yourself return to a more balanced state of awareness. If you notice that someone else is using any of these tactics against you, refuse to play the game. It is easy to get triggered and fight back, but it is also easy to say, "This doesn't feel right to me. Let me have a few moments to myself." Or if those words feel awkward, simply say, "Time out." If you are in a work situation where neither of these responses works, take the earliest opportunity to exit.

If you find yourself caught up in the game of pass it along with another person, a better intention doesn't always arise. It is often impossible to convert a bad emotional atmosphere into a happy one. It is equally hard, if you suddenly notice your own intentions going awry, to convert your negative feelings into positive ones. Don't place undue burdens on yourself. It isn't up to you to fix someone else or to make a bad situation better.

The one thing you can always do, however, is to take responsibility for your own feelings. This is the opposite of passing them along. You decide consciously not to adopt the tactics that do no one any good. By doing this, you give creative intelligence space to operate. The mental shift is conscious on your part, but it is creative intelligence that comes up with the emotions you need, which are part of the thoughts you think and the words you say. They are embedded with one another. You cannot reason out the right emotion for a situation. There is too much interference from the past to give you a clear perspective. Anyway, by the time you manage to figure out a particular emotion, the spontaneity of emotions has been lost, and, above all, emotions want to be spontaneous.

Trust is necessary at every level symbolized by the chakras, and this is certainly true for the heart chakra. The wisdom of emotions is a tremendous discovery, and it awaits you once you have the intention to discover it. Open a space for creative intelligence, and you will find that feeling your way through life is a great joy, just as it was always supposed to be.

ACTIVATING THE HEART CHAKRA

This chakra strengthens every aspect of mind but especially intuition, insight, and imagination. A few things you can do apply to every chakra in general:

- Be in simple awareness. When you notice that you aren't, take a few minutes to center yourself.
- Meditate on the mantra *Yam* (page 84).
- Meditate on the centering thought "I am love" or "I radiate love" (page 87).

Other steps are more specifically aimed at activating the heart chakra. Once you contact this seed of a loving or blissful emotion in your awareness, you can expand on it anytime you wish, which is the object of the following meditations.

Both meditations are performed sitting calmly alone in a quiet room without outside distractions. Prepare for the meditation by closing your eyes, taking a few deep breaths, and centering yourself.

MEDITATION #1

Take a moment to recall an experience in your past that brought you a feeling of pure joy and happiness. It can be an event as significant as a wedding or a birth, but it doesn't have to be. Perhaps a sunset over the sea or a piece of music is something you associate with an ecstatic feeling.

Relive the feeling by visualizing the experience as vividly as you can. Don't force the memories, but just let them appear naturally. As you do, notice your heart, where joy is felt physically. Place your attention on this heartfelt joy and sit with it for a few minutes before slowly opening your eyes. Keep your attention on the joyous feeling until it subsides on its own.

MEDITATION #2

Bliss-consciousness flows from the crown chakra to the heart, where it is experienced as warmth, love, and joy. A visualization of this is very helpful. Visualize a bright point of light just above the top of your head. Without forcing, see the point of light becoming more brilliant. When you have a clear image of this, let the light flow downward so that it gradually suffuses your heart.

A blue or white light is usually most effective. If it comes easily, see your heart made of light. Allow yourself to radiate brightly and outwardly. In this meditation, the feeling of bliss is like a side effect of the light. You don't have to reach for it as a feeling by itself.

CHAKRA 3

Powerful Action

THIRD CHAKRA

Location: *Solar plexus*

Theme: *Powerful action*

Desirable qualities:

   Physical health

   Willpower

   Determination

   Successful activity

For most people, real personal power seems like an impossibility. Many feel the opposite—that they have little control over where life takes them. The rush of change is everywhere, and modern life contains intricacies a previous generation never dreamed of. Amid the riot of human activity, the forces of Nature play themselves out indifferently, as they have for billions of years. Such a picture reduces you and me to mere specks, whose existence has no real consequence in the scheme of things.

The chakra system overturns this whole picture. It places personal power in the scheme of creative intelligence, whose power is infinite. In consciousness lies your strength, once you become aware of it. The third chakra, which is located at the level of the solar plexus above the navel, is known as the power chakra. Its energy is associated with action of every kind, including the motivation that drives it.

Creative intelligence knows the way to the successful conclusion of the goal you are aiming for. Successful action is Yoga's definition of personal power. Feeling weak, lonely, isolated, insignificant, and small is unreal from this new perspective. These feelings are symptoms of disconnection from your source.

Bliss-consciousness is more than a subjective experience—it connects you and the world. Thoughts, especially strong intentional thoughts, make things happen spontaneously. I'd be amazed if you buy into this idea already, but the best way to do this is to experiment with your everyday activity after you finish reading this chapter. If the flow of creative intelligence can truly accomplish things in the world "out there," then you are following your bliss into the so-called real world.

No doubt, it can often feel like you are powerless. But what you are actually experiencing during times of doubt, fear, and weakness is your response to the world. You feel powerless because your response is powerless. Keep up the same response, and the same feeling will persist. The third chakra can free you to be a powerful agent for change in your life, extending to everyone around you. Bliss should spill over into the world, like the Japanese custom of a host's generosity—the host fills his guest's glass until it overflows.

The third chakra is your power zone, where intention and fulfillment are connected automatically. By letting bliss-consciousness take over the whole process, you are free to follow your own vision, knowing that creative intelligence is on your side. As radical as that sounds, nothing is more secure than aligning your action with your vision.

IN THE ZONE

There is a specific set of conditions telling you that you are acting from the power chakra. These are well known in sports competition, and you've probably heard about being "in the zone." When a football player is in the zone, every pass is completed, not in the ordinary way, but as if it were happening on its own. The same is true of a golfer who lands a hole in one from 150 yards away. All the effort, practice, tension, and adrenaline that crowd into a competitive sport vanish, to be replaced by a completely different set of experiences.

Being in the zone isn't unique to sports, and our aim in this book is to make it a normal experience. You have almost certainly glimpsed how it feels to be in the zone without calling it that. The experience has the following elements:

- You are certain that you will succeed.
- You feel calm inside, but also wide awake and alert.
- All obstacles disappear.
- You feel a tingling energy in your body.
- You experience lightness of being.

- The action seems to be happening of its own accord.
- Time is likely to slow down or even seem to stop.
- You feel carefree and joyful.

These elements might seem alien to everyday life, but for most of us they were experienced under a special circumstance: falling in love. A wide receiver catching a long, spiraling pass in football doesn't seem like Romeo rhapsodizing under Juliet's balcony. But they are linked by bliss-consciousness. We are so used to separating "in here" and "out there" that a lover's ecstasy seems totally different from a football all-star leaping for the ball. But, in reality, there is only one power zone, whether we experience it "in here" or "out there." An infatuated lover occupies the zone as much as a professional athlete.

Unfortunately, everyone has more experience being out of the zone. The fact that we are so used to obstacles, setbacks, and failures testifies to creative intelligence getting blocked. There is a disconnect between what you really want and what you actually get. This has to change. Being in the zone is meant to be normal. All it requires is that the third chakra be open, allowing creative intelligence to flow through it. As we'll see, unblocking the third chakra happens through a shift in awareness, which is always possible.

OWN THE ZONE

Now you know the shift you need to make, letting creative intelligence take over every action. Action is a huge category, and whatever you undertake, the possibility of encountering accidents, mistakes, obstructions, and unforeseen consequences is always present. But the picture changes when you realize that simple awareness is all you need. By staying in simple awareness, you discover how to own the zone.

You are already familiar with what simple awareness feels like; it is characterized by inner calm, alertness, and relaxation. The trick is to remain in simple awareness while at the same time going through a day filled with demands, duties, and distractions. In the tradition of Yoga the ability to rest with complete confidence in simple awareness is highly valued, while in the West simple awareness has almost no place in daily life.

Instead, we are constantly told to focus on external factors. If you stick to the Western perspective, which is what countless people do, pressure and stress build up. This is inevitable because achieving success demands that you scatter your energies on many fronts. Can you really expect to keep up with all the following things?

- Maintaining a positive attitude

- Striving to be a winner instead of a loser

- Stoking your motivation and the motivation of those around you

- Seizing opportunity when it emerges

- Picking yourself up after setbacks

- Showing no fear or trepidation

- Keeping up your morale and bucking up the people around you

- Meeting the demand for hard work and struggle

Paying attention to all these things is essential to the mythology of success. By adopting this mythology as a way of life, success might follow, if not all the time, at least some of the time. But there's a major snag. The Western approach takes you out of the zone, and once this happens, you are guaranteed to stay out. Diving headlong into the struggle for success, by definition, keeps you in the struggle. In a game where the players are totally intent on winners and losers, what results in the long run is neither winning nor losing—the most common outcome is exhaustion and burnout. Too many people are walking around fatigued and stressed because they think this is the price they need to pay for a shot at success.

It is important to notice the signs that you are not in the zone, including the following:

- You are bored at work or even hate your job.

- Your life feels aimless.

- You are overwhelmed by a sense of futility. You think, "What does any of this matter anyway?"

- What you are doing requires exhausting effort and struggle, sapping your energy.

- You are uncertain about your next move.

- Your attention wanders; you get distracted easily.

- You find yourself trying too hard.

- You feel nervous and confused about the final outcome.

- You experience resistance and obstacles.

- You feel signs of stress, like tightness and tension in your body.

- You feel mentally burdened and anxious.

Let's assume that being out of the zone is the most common condition. Struggling against the symptoms listed above isn't Yoga's way. As you probably know by now, Yoga teaches only one necessity: *Get out of your own way.* Be in simple awareness so that creative intelligence can take over. Three things are involved: *witnessing, detachment,* and *nondoing.* Each comes naturally; you only have to pay attention to them and make them a meaningful part of your daily activity.

Note: To give you a personal experience of these three aspects of awareness, see the meditation at the end of this chapter.

Witnessing: When you are a witness to your actions, you are in the position of an observer. Without noticing it, everyone is already an observer, but in an erratic way. We cannot help but notice what we're doing, whether the action is as insignificant as walking to the refrigerator or as important as presiding over a board meeting. The observer is a necessary part of being self-aware—this isn't physical seeing through your eyes but consciously being aware of what you are doing.

Much of the time, however, people engage in habitual and unconscious action. They stay on autopilot, repeating the same old behavior—physically, mentally, and even spiritually. The witnessing element is pushed out of sight. Mechanical action takes over instead. When someone is in the zone, on the other hand, they feel as if they were standing outside themselves, observing their actions as if they were watching a movie or a dream. In essence, the witness replaces the ego.

In witnessing, the ego's default activity—liking and disliking, accepting and rejecting—fades away. A wider, deeper, more powerful force takes over, which is creative intelligence. It functions from much wider awareness than the ego possesses. You still have an intention, just as before, but you have it without losing self-awareness. As the witness, you see with perfect clarity what you are doing. It's like being engrossed in a movie and not paying attention to anything else in the room.

Detachment: This is experienced as letting go. When you are detached, you lose the *need* to force, struggle, push, and expend maximum effort. These are ego tactics, because the ego is out to get what it wants by whatever means necessary. When someone is in the zone, doing something remarkable under exceptional circumstances (e.g., a championship playoff or on the front line of battle), they report afterwards, "It wasn't me doing it." They are aware, in other words, of being in a state where an unnamable force has taken control.

The ego doesn't trust detachment, and since society is a collection of separate egos, none of us was raised to value it—quite the opposite. In the West, being detached is equated with passivity, indifference, and sitting on the sidelines while life passes you by. What this viewpoint overlooks is that detachment is totally necessary in order to remain alive and functioning. The central nervous system is divided by physiologists into two parts, the voluntary and involuntary nervous system. The voluntary system is under our conscious control; the involuntary system operates automatically, without choice on our part. The issue of being in control doesn't arise, and, as occupants of our bodies, we would be unable to take over in any case. A printed readout of every function occurring in your body at this minute would have to be a mile long, assuming that modern medicine could track them all.

Needing no intervention from us, creative intelligence is on display in the body to a miraculous extent, and the involuntary functions inside us are thrilled (if they could speak for themselves) that they don't have to put up with our meddling. Unfortunately, we do meddle. We subject ourselves to stress on a daily basis, which causes the involuntary nervous system to experience overload. Being highly adaptive, your body can adjust to being overloaded, but eventually a price must be paid, in the lasting effects of stress, aging, and the onset of chronic disease.

In those areas, the benefits of meditation are so well known that they hardly need mentioning, but it is worth knowing that the first benefit is to the involuntary nervous system. In meditation, you experience simple awareness, and your body experiences a state without stress. This period of relief and relaxation allows the healing response to begin to undo the ill effects of overload. The same applies to the voluntary nervous system. By giving the conscious mind a respite from constant grinding activity, a space is opened so that creative intelligence can enter the situation, bringing mental clarity, focused attention, relaxed awareness, and openness to new answers and solutions.

Once you comprehend the whole picture, detachment loses its negative connotations. You aren't indifferent and passive. Instead, you stop interfering so that creative intelligence can do what it is designed to do.

Non-doing: Life, we have been taught, is all about doing, so right off the bat the term *non-doing* sounds lazy and suspicious, if not impossible to carry out. If you stop doing, nothing can result but stasis and stagnation. However, non-doing is actually a path to increased success in the actions you take. This needs explaining.

When you are in the zone, great things can get accomplished, but that's not the main reason for being there. The main reason is to reconnect with bliss-consciousness. As long as you remain connected, creative intelligence operates fully, allowing you to stop interfering with life. You feel no need to—things happen smoothly on their own. You find yourself making choices without stress, pressure, or demands. Doing whatever you please leads to the most fruitful and successful outcome.

As you might imagine, your ego will have none of it. It will throw up red flags everywhere: *How can you possibly survive, much less succeed, if you simply stand aside and trust in this so-called creative intelligence, which might be a fiction of a mystical imagination?* The ego's objection sounds reasonable, but only because the ego sees life from its own narrow perspective. It is deprived of simple awareness, since life at the ego level is all about "What's in it for me?" There is a constant preoccupation with desires and needs, even if the needs are imaginary.

Simple awareness doesn't work this way. Witnessing, detachment, and non-doing aren't an agenda; you don't set out to attain them. They are aspects of simple awareness. They exist in you as part of "I am enough." To comprehend this fully, you need the experience of non-doing to know that it is part of you, just as you need to experience detachment and witnessing. This is where the path of self-awareness comes in, to reconnect you to who you really are.

FINDING THE PATH

The ego has selfishness on its side, which is a powerful motivator. But nothing your ego achieves will allow you to be in the zone. Yet people cannot be blamed for following where the ego leads. A small voice might whisper about finding a better way, but this better way doesn't just magically appear. A journey based on "I am not enough" ends up with unfulfilled promise, no matter how well you have lived.

I recently ran across a poignant example of this lesson. In a small Austrian village about twenty miles outside Vienna, the widow of a local magistrate sat alone in her empty house. Her name was Marianne Berchtold, and she was born into a musical family in 1751. For years the elderly Marianne, known in childhood as Nannerl, had been in declining health. A visitor in 1829 described her as "blind, languid, exhausted, feeble, and nearly speechless."

If you are a music lover, you might know that Mozart had an older sister nicknamed Nannerl, and lonely Frau Berchtold used to be her. She had been one half of the most famous duo of child prodigies in music history because, by some miracle, the Mozart family had produced two prodigies. At eight, Nannerl was an exquisitely talented pianist. She would have been considered remarkable, able to outplay many adults at the keyboard, except that Wolfgang was an even greater wonder.

At four, he had begun to play all the pieces Nannerl could play, but, in addition, he started composing at five and could improvise on any tune handed to him. He could memorize long pieces on sight, and when their father, Leopold, took them on tour, Wolfgang loved to perform a trick.

Someone would cover the keyboard of a piano or harpsichord with a cloth, and the child prodigy would play perfectly under the cloth without seeing the keyboard.

It is hard to connect the blind, nearly mute Marianne with a girl who had almost, as a performer, been Mozart's equal. She had been admired by the kings and queens of Europe, receiving lavish gifts from every noble house the Mozart children played before, which numbered in the hundreds. Nannerl and Wolfgang had an affectionate relationship, although it seems that they lost touch before his tragic early death, at thirty-five, in 1786. She outlived him by almost forty years but had no performing life after her childhood.

As extraordinary as her circumstances were, she wound up wasting her gifts and became imprisoned by limitation. If we could pull Nannerl Mozart into our own time, the worst circumstances would be drastically improved. In eighteenth-century Vienna, women could not become professional musicians. Today Nannerl could have made a career for herself. Society would give her choices beyond obeying her father and then being tied to a petty magistrate in total obscurity. Best of all, she could have had a comfortable old age, probably free of blindness if she had cataracts or glaucoma, the two most common causes of lost eyesight, both now treatable. (How Mozart died remains unknown, but the best guess is rheumatic fever, now easily curable with antibiotics.)

Once you improve all these distressing circumstances, the path of self-awareness would be just as hidden today as it was in the eighteenth century. Musical talent is a gift from creative intelligence, but it doesn't change the person's state of awareness. If you had a magic wand and could wave away every external woe, you would not free someone from being trapped in mind-made prisons.

Freeing yourself from mind-made prison is up to you. Lifting yourself above "I am not enough" is your first and most important project. The Mozart children had the good fortune to be showered with gold by rich patrons. Your good fortune lies in the fact that no matter how well or badly life has treated you, the hidden path was never denied you. In all its purity, it remains as accessible as ever.

Yoga offers a universal vision of the human condition by opening up every possibility. The hidden path is activated when you follow a vision by being aware of where you want to go. Here is what Yoga's vision looks like, couched in words that apply to everyone.

A Vision You Can Live By

- The true measure of success is joy.

- Being in the zone is normal.

- Waking up is a constant process.

- Your reality is created in your awareness.

- Life is a field of infinite possibilities.

- Every day should bring more fulfillment.

- Effort and struggle are unnecessary.

- There is a path out of pain and suffering.

Most of these axioms sound familiar, because I've applied them as each chakra shows a new transformation of bliss-consciousness. Now we've reached the level of action, which brings bliss into the workaday world of family, friends, work, and relationships. No matter how many demands the world "out there" puts on you, you can live by your vision. Let me turn vision into practicality so that clear choices can be made starting now.

EVOLVE EVERY DAY

It's no secret that life is dynamic—all of us are tossed around by change. In itself, change is meaningless. A rock left out in the elements will eventually be worn down to dust by wind and rain. It took about two billion years before the basic elements in a rock, along with the elements of wind and water, found a way to evolve beyond chaos. The solution is what we call life, because living things use the raw stuff of planet Earth to evolve. Evolution is the pushback that defeats chaos.

This was true billions of years ago and remains true now, but at a much higher level. Human beings can consciously evolve. No matter how many wonderful gadgets we invent and incredible discoveries we make, all of which signify progress, all evolution begins in awareness. Everything comes down to personal evolution and the choice to evolve every day.

You can evolve today by making choices that overcome disorder, chaos, and dysfunction. Here are a few examples:

- Take a step to reduce stress at home or at work.

- Make your immediate surroundings calm and orderly.

- Stop doing one thing that you know isn't good for you.

- Start doing one thing that you know is good for you.

- Give priority to your inner life.

- Find a source of inspiration.

- Increase your contact with someone who uplifts you.

- Decrease your contact with someone who discourages or mistreats you.

- Help uplift someone else.

REVERSE THE ENTROPY

Life is meant to flow smoothly, without struggles and resistance. When you meet with struggle and resistance, energy gets drained away. In physics, this is known as entropy. If you do not make choices that keep your energy fresh and renewed, you are giving in to entropy. Everyone knows how it feels when a situation or a person drains them on the emotional level. Energy drain goes beyond high-maintenance relationships, however. It goes beyond a busy day that leaves you feeling tired and depleted.

The real damage is that entropy is the opposite of evolution. You can't evolve when you are preoccupied with keeping disorder and chaos at bay, when you are struggling to get through the day without exhaustion, and when stress is constant, even low-level stress. In physics, entropy mainly applies to the tendency in Nature for heat to disperse and reach an even level, but in human affairs we want to have renewed energy every day at the mental, emotional, and physical level.

To reduce entropy and encourage renewal, here are some suggestions:

- Keep your workload within your comfort zone.

- Take time to stretch and move every hour.

- Don't perform any activity to the point of feeling tired.

- Sit and briefly relax several times a day.

- Don't depend on coffee or other stimulants.

- Focus on getting enough sleep that you feel refreshed in the morning.

- Avoid situations that predictably lead to arguments.

- Ask everyone in the family to share chores. Don't martyr yourself by taking on the responsibility for things someone else should be doing.

- Break up any activity that is boring, routine, or stale. Ideally, minimize such activities as much as you can.

- Take stress reduction seriously.

- Avoid people who make you feel drained.

STAY CLOSE TO THE SOURCE

As you undertake any activity, creative intelligence flows into the activity. Creative intelligence is strongest at the source, so your actions—whatever they are—should keep you close to the source. Whenever you are deeply absorbed in something, that's a sign that you are close to the source. Creative activity keeps you close to the source, as does meditation. Brain activity looks very similar in both. Whenever you feel blissful, uplifted, joyous, or buoyant, that's another sign. Value this state of awareness and stay in it. The active mind tends to have a hair trigger—any distraction will tend to disrupt the state of quiet but intense focus of being close to the source. Your aim should be to experience being close to the source every day.

Here are a few suggestions to guide you:

- Focus on one thing at a time. Don't try to multitask.

- If you notice yourself losing focus, pause and rest for a few minutes with your eyes closed.

- Make time to do something creative every day.

- Reflect on what really brings joy to you personally and make time for it.

- Take up regular meditation or yoga.

- Take time to be absorbed in the beauty of nature.

- Ask others to give you uninterrupted time for part of the day so that you can pursue focused activity.

- Turn off your smartphone for at least half an hour a day. Keep it off during focused or creative activity.

- Don't be dependent on activity that makes your mind lazy and passive, such as couch-potato TV watching.

EXPAND YOUR POSSIBILITIES

At your source is the field of infinite possibilities. Humans enjoy an open-ended existence because life's possibilities are never exhausted. But there are strong pressures, both internal and external, to severely limit the possibilities someone is able to experience. The pressure to conform, the desire not to be an outsider, repressed feelings, and groupthink exert their inhibiting influence. The average person might not compose forty pieces of music a year the way Franz Schubert did (at almost twice the rate of Mozart), or equal Thomas Edison's total of 1,093 patents, much less write more than two thousand published works, as did Voltaire and a dozen other writers in history. But creative intelligence exists to expand, explore, know, and discover. This is different from obsession, which depends on repetition, leads to exhaustion, and lacks the feeling of enjoyment. Expanding your possibilities every day brings vibrancy to your life; the direction you take is up to you.

Here are some suggestions to guide you:

- Undertake a long-range challenging project, such as learning a foreign language.

- Expose yourself to challenging ideas.

- Engage in an activity that stretches your boundaries, such as community or charity work.

- Engage in volunteer work that brings you into contact with people who are different from you in race, education, or social class, for example.

- Set out to earn a college or advanced degree.

- Listen to a podcast or attend a lecture that plants the seed of a new interest.

- Steer conversations away from gossip or the exchange of idle opinions, raising an actual topic for discussion.

- Find a confidant with whom you can share your deepest thoughts and feelings.

- Become a mentor.

As you can see, having a vision—and carrying it out every day—is the highest and best use of activity. It keeps the flow of creative intelligence alive. We cannot tell, observing from the outside, if animals experience life as vibrant and joyous. In turn, they cannot tell how humans are set apart by our open-ended existence. Yet, it is certain that we are designed to experience existence as something constantly dynamic and evolutionary. Personal growth is a uniquely human possibility. Take advantage of this possibility every day, and you will be in the zone, empowered by creative intelligence as your normal way of being.

ACTIVATING THE SOLAR PLEXUS CHAKRA

This chakra strengths every aspect of action, but especially the connection between intention and outcome. A few things you can do apply to every chakra in general:

- Be in simple awareness. When you notice that you aren't, take a few minutes to center yourself.
- Meditate on the mantra *Ram* (page 84).
- Meditate on the centering thought "I am in my power" or "I am empowerment" (page 87).

Other steps are more specifically aimed at activating your power chakra. Yoga is very explicit about how a desire comes true at the level of intention. You bypass the ego's state of unending desire, which is preoccupied with repeating pleasant experiences from the past. These bubble up all the time and block your view of deeper awareness.

Below the chattering mind, having an intention can be connected to fulfilling the intention, according to Yoga, through a skill known as *Samyama*. This is the Sanskrit term for "holding" or "tying together." In this case you are holding together an intention and the result it procures. Samyama involves three ingredients merged into one. All three exist in your normal thinking process without carrying much power. The power comes from deepening the process.

When you go more deeply than the surface activity of the mind, this is known as *Samadhi*.

When you have a strong intention in mind, this is known
as *Dharana*.
When you stay focused and await what happens, this is
known as *Dhyana*.

Leaving aside the Sanskrit terms, the important thing
is that Samyama is as natural as your everyday thinking
and desiring. If you play the cello or can make a perfect chocolate soufflé, you go to the level of awareness
where this skill exists, you stay there with focused attention, and you specify what you want to accomplish.

Being skilled at Samyama develops naturally from
simple awareness the more you practice it, and you can
deepen this through mantra meditation. It is *Samadhi*,
the level of awareness you can reach, that presents
probably the greatest challenge. You can't simply say to
yourself, "I want to go deeper." Just saying the words
isn't enough. There is no startling experience to be had
until Samadhi becomes so profound in your consciousness that time and ego vanish, placing you very close to
the eternal silence at the very foundation of awareness.

You can get better at Samyama by following a few
pointers:

- Find time once or twice a day for mantra
  meditation that lasts fifteen to twenty minutes.
- At the end of a satisfying meditation, consciously
  see something you'd like to have happen. Then
  be alert to how this intention might be working out.

- In activity, when you experience a moment of quiet mind, settle into it, rather than letting it pass.
- When something good comes your way without effort on your part, notice this and silently say, "This is working," meaning the path of self-awareness.
- Be easy on yourself, whether you are experiencing success or setbacks. The burden is not on you. Creative intelligence is working through you as best it can.
- Don't be so eager to run after your ego's demands and desires. Take some downtime every day. Be appreciative of the natural world. Settle inside yourself whenever you have a free moment to enjoy the experience.

CHAKRA 2

The Path of Desire

SECOND CHAKRA

Location: Lower back (sacrum)

Theme: Fulfilled desire

Desirable qualities:

> Five senses
>
> Physical desires
>
> Sensuality, sexuality

There are many paths in life, but no matter what path you are on, it is a path of desire. Desire motivates us to pursue what we want. Even if you are an ascetic, whose aim is to renounce all worldly desires, that goal—let's say renunciation to gain total inner peace—is something you want. You are following a desire, just as certainly as a toddler reaching for a piece of candy. No motivation is stronger or more persistent than desire.

Desire has an important place in the chakra system, too. The fulfillment of desire is the purpose of the second chakra, which is located in the lower back or sacrum. Here bliss-consciousness is transformed into the five senses, along with sensual and sexual pleasure. A basic teaching of Yoga says that desire is rooted in the senses. Nobody really has to be told this. We spend our days looking, hearing, touching, tasting, and smelling. What the senses find appealing draws us closer to a person, object, or pursuit. What the senses find unappealing is often a sign to move in the opposite direction.

The ego derives power from desire. "I want this" and "I don't want that" keeps life humming along at the ego level. If you free yourself from the ego's agenda, however, desire shifts its purpose. Instead of boosting the separate, isolated self, desire becomes about bliss. The trajectory of your desires would look like this:

Blissful impulse ⟶ *Blissful action* ⟶ *Blissful result*

When the beginning and end of a process are joined together, you have Yoga, or union. There's nothing exotic or mystical here. A mother wants to cradle her newborn baby, she picks the baby up, and she commences to rock her child back and forth in her arms. The experience begins with a blissful impulse, proceeds to blissful action, and leads to a blissful result.

Right now, the path of desire in almost everyone's life is dictated by the ego, with its endless wants, needs, impulsiveness, and craving. Instead of bliss, the experience begins with lack: "I don't have what I want." When desire is based on bliss-consciousness instead, you are motivated by wanting the expansion of bliss. This is why "Follow your bliss" isn't worded as "Follow your next craving."

BLISSFUL DESIRES

The things you favor in your life will grow, and whatever you ignore will wither on the vine. You have a choice to favor any impulse, which means you can favor your blissful desires. You don't have to force or control the process. A simple shift of attention is all you need. You are expressing a blissful impulse whenever you

Show your love and affection.

Offer appreciation to someone else.

Soothe another person's pain and suffering.

Act selflessly, through generous giving.

Search for knowledge.

Do the right thing.

Speak your truth.

Nurture a child.

Offer hope and encouragement.

Inspire yourself and those around you.

By favoring these desires, you align yourself with the flow of creative intelligence. In common parlance, we talk about "selfless" acts, but it is impossible to eliminate the self, and you wouldn't want to. The self is your avenue for personal growth. Blissful desires should be called "egoless," because you are shifting away from the ego's agenda. If you followed your ego's desires all the time, nobody else would matter. You'd ignore those in need; you would feel no desire to protect the weak, help the suffering, or comfort someone in times of distress.

Thankfully, there is another dimension to desire that includes other people, kindness, and compassion. By favoring those impulses, you will escape the insecurity and neediness of the ego. There is no substitute for the experience of bliss and letting it guide you in your personal growth.

NEED VERSUS WANT

Of course, not all desires, wishes, and dreams come true. Much of the time, your disappointment is seemingly beyond your control. You want a job but don't get it; you run a race and don't come in first; you long for the ideal romantic partner, but he or she doesn't appear. The number of times we don't get what we want sticks in our memory and strongly influences how we approach the whole issue of desire.

In the Yoga tradition, nothing can be denied to you if your desire is supported by dharma. What's wrong with merely wanting what you want? Wanting what you want may not coincide with what you need, and dharma supports everything you need, not every desire that flits through your mind. In addition, the act of merely wanting something is superficial most of the time, a flicker of desire mixed in with the constant hum of mental activity.

This explanation isn't a sly way to justify unfulfilled desires. If you want something but don't get it, nobody—not even an advanced yogi or guru—has the right to tell you that you went about the process the wrong way, and therefore the failure is your fault. When you are in simple awareness, fewer pointless desires float into your mind. Because you are aligned with creative intelligence, you are much more likely to have intentions that address a real need. These desires are the kind that have the greatest chance of coming true.

Red flags might be going up at this point. As children, we got into the habit of saying "I want" as a repeated habit, which caused our parents to frown and reply, "That's not something you really need." In this way *need* became a word that fights against desire. However, being restricted to bare necessities isn't the way to have a good life (though, strictly speaking, nobody needs anything but a few serviceable clothes, a basic nutritious diet, and a roof over their head).

Need must be reframed to get past this negative connotation. The bare necessities call up scarcity, rather than abundance. Moreover, most people think in terms of material needs when a child's need for love is a genuine necessity that doesn't go away in adulthood. Emotional and psychological needs are the most overlooked, and the most abused, in our society. In Yoga, a need can be defined as anything that helps you experience bliss and promote inner growth, or evolution.

As the chakra of desire, the second chakra brings fulfillment in abundance, not just the bare necessities. Abundance pours out like generous Providence in the New Testament. However, getting every little thing you want is a childish fantasy. Desires are fulfilled based on what the Eightfold Path in Buddhism calls "right mindfulness." If we break this phrase down, *mindfulness* is about being present and living in the moment. The word *right* indicates that you must remain aware of the dharma—the flow of creative intelligence that brings what you need.

Ideally, there is nothing else to do, but this is true only when your journey has arrived at enlightenment, where simple awareness is your constant state. Meanwhile, you can improve your results by separating wants from needs. The two often overlap, which is only natural. When you think, "I really need a vacation," you are also expressing a want. But if you are enticing somebody to do what you want, saying, "I really need you to do this for me," it is likely to be what you want, not what you really need. Of course, there are many ways in which we need friends, but manipulating them crosses the line. Creative intelligence sorts the situation out better than the thinking mind ever could.

You have to experience this for yourself before it can become your truth. The following quiz will help you see how you stand with the needs that are supported by the second chakra.

QUIZ

How Well Are You Meeting Your Needs?

Everyone is supported by creative intelligence. The only difference is how much support you are actually getting. This is the critical issue. Bliss-consciousness aims to support you 100 percent. As you learn to be in simple awareness more and more, your support will steadily increase.

It's worthwhile to see where you stand now. For each item listed below, you will be asked two things:

- **How important is this need to you?**
  Answer on a scale from 1 to 10, where 1 = Not at all important and 10 = Most important.

- **How well are you meeting this need?**
  Answer *Poorly, Fairly Well,* or *Very Well.*

Think about this quiz as a self-assessment, not a test. There are no right answers for everyone, since we assess our needs quite personally.

PART 1: LIFE NEEDS

This section is about the seven most important needs that arise in everyone's life.

1. I need to feel safe and secure.
   How important is this need to you, **from 1 to 10?** _____
   How well are you meeting this need?
      Poorly ☐   **Fairly** ☐   **Well** ☐   **Very Well** ☐

2. I need to have some success and achievement I can be proud of.
   How important is this need to you, **from 1 to 10?** _____
   How well are you meeting this need?
      Poorly ☐   **Fairly** ☐   **Well** ☐   **Very Well** ☐

3. I need to have a family or other close support system.
   How important is this need to you, **from 1 to 10?** _____
   How well are you meeting this need?
      Poorly ☐   **Fairly** ☐   **Well** ☐   **Very Well** ☐

4. I need to be accepted and understood.
   How important is this need to you, **from 1 to 10?** _____
   How well are you meeting this need?
      Poorly ☐   **Fairly** ☐   **Well** ☐   **Very Well** ☐

5. I need a creative outlet.
   How important is this need to you, **from 1 to 10?** _____
   How well are you meeting this need?
      Poorly ☐   **Fairly** ☐   **Well** ☐   **Very Well** ☐

6. I need something larger than myself to believe in—a higher value system, faith, or a spiritual tradition.

How important is this need to you, **from 1 to 10?** _____
How well are you meeting this need?

   Poorly ☐   Fairly ☐   Well ☐   Very Well ☐

7. I need to be on the journey to higher consciousness and personal growth.

How important is this need to you, **from 1 to 10?** _____
How well are you meeting this need?

   Poorly ☐   Fairly ☐   Well ☐   Very Well ☐

PART 2: RELATIONSHIP NEEDS

These are needs that are part of a satisfying relationship. (You can answer based on your experiences, even if you aren't in a relationship right now.)

8. I need to feel wanted by my partner.

How important is this need to you, **from 1 to 10?** _____
How well are you meeting this need?

   Poorly ☐   Fairly ☐   Well ☐   Very Well ☐

9. I need to feel safe with my partner.

How important is this need to you, **from 1 to 10?** _____
How well are you meeting this need?

   Poorly ☐   Fairly ☐   Well ☐   Very Well ☐

10. I need to trust my partner and be trusted in return.

How important is this need to you, **from 1 to 10?** _____
How well are you meeting this need?

   Poorly ☐   Fairly ☐   Well ☐   Very Well ☐

11. I need to have warmth and affection.

How important is this need to you, **from 1 to 10?** _____

How well are you meeting this need?

    Poorly ☐   **Fairly** ☐   **Well** ☐   **Very Well** ☐

12. I need to have a fulfilling sex life.

How important is this need to you, **from 1 to 10?** _____

How well are you meeting this need?

    Poorly ☐   **Fairly** ☐   **Well** ☐   **Very Well** ☐

13. I need to feel respect for my partner and be respected in return.

How important is this need to you, **from 1 to 10?** _____

How well are you meeting this need?

    Poorly ☐   **Fairly** ☐   **Well** ☐   **Very Well** ☐

14. I need close physical contact.

How important is this need to you, **from 1 to 10?** _____

How well are you meeting this need?

    Poorly ☐   **Fairly** ☐   **Well** ☐   **Very Well** ☐

15. I need my own space whenever I ask for it.

How important is this need to you, **from 1 to 10?** _____

How well are you meeting this need?

    Poorly ☐   **Fairly** ☐   **Well** ☐   **Very Well** ☐

16. I need the freedom to follow my own path.

How important is this need to you, **from 1 to 10?** _____

How well are you meeting this need?

    Poorly ☐   **Fairly** ☐   **Well** ☐   **Very Well** ☐

17. I need children who feel loved by me and my partner.

How important is this need to you, **from 1 to 10?** _____

How well are you meeting this need?

    Poorly ☐   **Fairly** ☐   **Well** ☐   **Very Well** ☐

18. I need my partner to be a success.

How important is this need to you, **from 1 to 10?** ____

How well are you meeting this need?

Poorly ☐   **Fairly** ☐   **Well** ☐   **Very Well** ☐

19. I need my children to make me proud.

How important is this need to you, **from 1 to 10?** ____

How well are you meeting this need?

Poorly ☐   **Fairly** ☐   **Well** ☐   **Very Well** ☐

20. I need to feel that I am the most important person in my partner's life.

How important is this need to you, **from 1 to 10?** ____

How well are you meeting this need?

Poorly ☐   **Fairly** ☐   **Well** ☐   **Very Well** ☐

ASSESSING YOUR RESULTS

If your answers are mostly **strong positives (Very Well)**, you enjoy very good support for your needs. You are aligned with the flow of creative intelligence, even if you don't think in those terms yet. Your everyday life is characterized by clear intentions, a lack of self-doubt, and the ability to know what you truly value.

This isn't the same as rating each need highly (7 to 10). You know yourself well enough to give low ratings to things that don't matter very much to you. Yet there is room for reflection. Look at the needs you don't find important and ask yourself if there is an aspect of your life, such as finding a creative outlook or needing warmth and affection, that you should look at more closely.

If you give **mostly average (Fairly Well)** answers, your needs are being fulfilled here and there. There are probably some that you have given up on, but the general problem is that you have low expectations. For you, the key thing is to feel that you deserve more and better. By having that intention, you can take steps, even small ones, toward getting more out of life. Begin with things that aren't threatening, such as finding a creative outlet. If your rating of your relationship needs is only fair, sit down with your partner and show him or her your results. It also helps to have your partner take the test so that you can have a shared basis for looking at where your relationship stands.

If you gave consistently **low (Poorly)** answers on the quiz, your needs are not being met the way they should be. There might be many reasons for this, including self-doubt, an unsatisfying relationship, or the struggle to meet basic necessities. For you, the best way forward is to sit down with someone you trust and admire, and go over your answers together. You need to begin to feel more supported in your life. This can be a tough road, but at the level of creative intelligence, you have access to support inside yourself that you can count on. Right now, this might not feel very real. Just take one or two needs where you are already doing well and set the intention that they will improve even more. The essential thing is that you need to meet yourself at a deeper level of awareness where answers and solutions are found.

Right now you are likely to be meeting yourself at the level of worry, confusion, and doubt. The state of simple awareness can give you a way to escape this level in order to find inner calm and peace.

PLEASURE OR BLISS?

As alluded to earlier, the second chakra is the seat of the five senses. There is no doubt that the five senses bring us pleasure. Who doesn't want to see beautiful things, listen to lovely music, and taste good food? The other side of the coin are finger-wagging moralists who lecture us about overindulgence. Add religion to the mix and the sensuous life is often equated with sin (the seven deadly sins, for example, begin with lust and gluttony, which are sensual sins).

Modern people have largely turned their backs on the old-fashioned moralism that looked upon innocent activities like dancing as an offense against God. In their place, sensual pleasure has run into different problems, those of excess. One way to see this is by looking at cravings and addictions. They are extreme cases where the five senses have no connection with bliss. Instead, pleasure is forced into doing something it cannot do, namely, end pain and suffering. If you eat your feelings, you are asking the pleasurable taste of food to bring you emotional comfort. If you use alcohol or drugs to escape into a zone free of stress and distress, you are asking a chemical to substitute for healing. What cravings and addictions have in common are two things. The first is repetition. Eating one piece of chocolate or drinking one glass of wine leads to a second, then a third, and so on.

Repetition is a sign that food, alcohol, drugs, or other addictive habits are being used as a psychological crutch. The mind has plugged into repeated hits of pleasure to dull, numb, or escape the underlying issue, which is usually anxiety. But the tactic is futile in the end because of diminishing returns—this is the second thing that cravings and addictions have in common. What begins as a pleasurable sensation starts to be less effective, and eventually obsession takes over. The habit feeds on itself without giving any pleasure, until the only use someone finds in overeating, drinking to excess, or getting stoned is keeping down the pain.

People excessively crave sex, drugs, food, and alcohol because they have no access to bliss. This is the hidden message in the chakra system. Several truths are contained in the message, so let's unpack them.

Deeper Truths About Desire

- What you truly desire isn't a thing—it is the feeling of fulfillment.

- The ultimate fulfillment is bliss, joy, and ecstasy.

- You already have bliss at the source.

- When you pursue any desire, you are actually trying to recapture what you already have inside you.

- Expand your awareness, and the fulfillment of desire will naturally follow.

Access to bliss is everything. The fulfillment of desire exists at the beginning and continues through all the steps that make the desire come true. This, we might say, is the ultimate win/win. The *Bhagavad Gita* says, "Perform action without regard for the fruits of action." For centuries this axiom has seemed utterly baffling. It appears to say that we should undertake our daily activities and follow our desires without caring whether these lead to success or failure. This goes against the grain of Western culture, where people are "in it to win it." Who would play baseball if winning and losing were both the same? Who would ask for a raise at work and feel equally contented if the raise were denied?

But this is a misreading. The seers who wrote the *Gita* were addressing a reader who is experiencing simple awareness as the starting point for every desire and action. If you already experience bliss, then you find yourself not needing more. You carry out your daily activity and pursue your desires, not for personal gain, but because creative intelligence knows that they are needed. Think of two mothers with newborn babies, one mother experiencing simple awareness, the other fretting about how her baby is doing. Both would still care for their child. It's a necessary action. Being in simple awareness doesn't change this fact. Yet the two mothers are having different experiences. Think of how much better it is to be a blissful mother than one who is worried and fretting. Placing consciousness first unfolds the best path in all situations.

Yet societies around the world make a different choice. As long as the goal is pleasure, the reward is short term at best. Everyone needs to learn that creative intelligence is already working in their lives. It's just a matter of aligning your desires with the creative intelligence that is always present.

DHARMA AND RELATIONSHIPS

You share your life with everyone around you in small and large ways. Your fulfillment is woven into the fulfillment of family, friends, and co-workers. In a word, life is about relationships. So how do you nurture your relationships in a way supported by dharma? As much as we love the people closest to us, conflicts arise. Person A wants one thing, Person B another. If you take the conflict down to the ego level, there is rarely a satisfying conclusion. Someone will emerge from the conflict feeling frustrated. This is how a relationship descends into futile arguments that bring nobody a sense of satisfaction. Yet at the level of creative intelligence, there is always a path to shared fulfillment. It would be ideal if everyone acted on this knowledge, but we are far from the ideal.

Because you understand how creative intelligence works, you also know the value of getting out of the way. Let simple awareness be your home base. Outcomes that your ego cannot achieve come naturally to creative intelligence, because it always operates from the level of the solution instead of the level of the problem.

In everyday situations, getting out of the way begins by giving up on the ego's fantasies. Your ego harbors childish and selfish dreams of getting what it wants all the time, by whatever means necessary. Even if you hold yourself back from extreme selfish behavior, you are under the influence of these futile fantasies, generally without knowing it. If you look at a relationship that isn't going well—with family, friends, or in an intimate relationship—almost certainly you or the other person is acting out a fantasy the ego has concocted and is stubbornly holding on to for dear life.

FIVE FANTASIES THAT CRIPPLE RELATIONSHIPS

Our deepest desires—to be loved, accepted, and understood—draw us into relationships. Look around at the relationships in your life that are working well. One or more of these deep desires is being satisfied. There is a best friend you can say anything to without being judged. There is a spouse or partner ready to forgive. In the chakra scheme, we'd say that the flow of creative intelligence is open.

Now look around at the relationships in your life that

bring frustration. Here there is no easy flow of love, understanding, and acceptance. Instead the ego is indulging in tactics that don't work, leading to deeper frustration and disagreement. Why do we stubbornly stick with behavior that clearly isn't working, that brings mutual misery? The answer is that we are choosing fantasy over reality. Let me get down to specifics, and I think you will find it easier to see yourself in the mirror.

FANTASY #1: "YOU NEED TO LISTEN TO ME. MEANWHILE, I REFUSE TO LISTEN TO YOU."

When two opposing sides stop listening to each other, the relationship has reached an impasse. Communication has shut down. In its place, rigid rituals are acted out. These rituals consist of repeating the same argument over and over again, shouting to try to be heard, and freezing the other person out with rude contempt or silence.

FANTASY #2: "EVERYTHING WILL BE OKAY IF YOU CHANGE. I CERTAINLY DON'T NEED TO CHANGE."

This is the classic disguise for blame. When you demand that the other person change, you are judging yourself against them without really coming out and saying so. What fuels this fantasy is the delusion that someone else will change if you blame them enough. Adding to this fantasy is a self-righteous confidence that you don't need to change because the other person has no right to blame you.

FANTASY #3: "YOU ARE HERE TO MAKE ME HAPPY. UNTIL YOU DO THAT, I CAN'T RELATE TO YOU."

This fantasy is a holdover from childhood. Young children pout and cry when they are unhappy, and as long as they are unhappy, they don't relate. They are too sunk in their own feelings. When carried over into adulthood, the same attitude becomes narcissistic. Other people exist to make you happy, and unless they realize this, you won't relate to them. Much of the time you are merely using them.

FANTASY #4: "I'M BETTER THAN YOU. THAT'S WHY I HAVE THE RIGHT TO TELL YOU WHAT TO DO."

Much of social discord can be attributed to a mutual superiority complex. Tune in on television to commentators for the other side in politics from yours, and you will probably be shocked (or not so shocked) at their sense of superiority to you, especially if you think that only your side has the right to feel superior. In relationships, the message is generally more covert, but when two people insist, "I'm right," there's a hint of feeling superior peeking through.

FANTASY #5: "I DESERVE TO WIN AND, ONCE I DO, YOU WILL BE SUNK ONCE AND FOR ALL."

This is the emotional equivalent of a zero-sum game. The Super Bowl is a zero-sum game, because only one side can win. But human affairs are tidal. One day you are down, the next day you are up. The belief that you can be up forever and never down again is pure fantasy.

If two people, two factions, or two nations find themselves stuck at an angry impasse, these five fantasies are almost always in play. Perhaps not all of them at once, and perhaps not everyone is honest about how they feel, yet this makes no difference. Each fantasy is based on two underlying tendencies. The first tendency is holding judgments; the second is us-versus-them thinking. These tendencies are not innate; you have to be taught them. And that means you can unlearn them. This opens the way for change.

CREATIVE CHANGE

Once you have looked in the mirror and grasped how your ego fantasies are working against you, you can take steps to change your thinking and behavior. Discard the blame that makes the other person wrong. That person doesn't have to change to make you happy—the responsibility for improving a relationship falls on the one who is motivated to create change. The responsibility becomes joyful when your motivation shifts away from ego toward letting creative intelligence deliver the outcome that is best for you and the other person. Let us look more closely at the theme of getting out of the way.

No matter what kind of disagreement arises in your relationship, the other person is putting up arguments, resistance, and obstacles. This boils down to saying no. You want to get to yes, which is also the goal of creative intelligence. Here is how to get there.

Turning No to Yes

- Give up on controlling, demanding, or persuading the other person.

- Sit down in a state of rational calmness. The other person needs to be calm and receptive, too. If that's not the case, postpone things until both sides are in a receptive state of mind.

- Show respect for the other person's position.

- Do more listening than talking.

- Be prepared for compromise.

- Drop us-versus-them thinking.

- Look for win/win options.

- Don't display anger and impatience.

- Find a place of nonjudgment inside yourself.

- Don't quit until both sides are satisfied.

The general theme is this: When someone else is blocking what you want, take responsibility for your behavior—it's much easier than trying to change the other person. You put yourself in the position of letting creative intelligence bring about a solution, a choice no one else has to join in.

The principles for getting to yes are well known in diplomatic circles, but they are flouted in everyday life. We all fall back on tactics that hardly ever work or, when they seem to work, leave residues of resentment in the other person. In practical terms, check to see if you are doing any of the following—they are more or less guaranteed to prevent you from getting what you want.

How People Get Stuck on No

- Insisting on blaming and complaining

- Dismissing the other person's viewpoint

- Entering into discussion when you are angry and upset

- Making the other person out to be your enemy

- Talking about differences rather than points of agreement

- Trying to win while making the other person lose

- Listing your demands and refusing to back down

- Walking away angry, with nothing settled

Arguments between couples and whole nations bring out these self-defeating behaviors, and yet we resort to them over and over at the urging of the ego. When you see them listed, you have no trouble in the cold light of day seeing how unproductive they are. It is worth the time to sit down and reflect on the list and how it applies to the last argument you had or the last time somebody blocked you from getting what you wanted. Getting what you want is a natural impulse, but using the wrong means to do so leads to frustration and futility.

Desire opens the most natural path to any goal, simply because wanting something badly enough is such a powerful motivator. The second chakra motivates you to win more and more bliss, and it motivates you to escape a life without bliss. My view is that the first motivation—to win more and more bliss—works better, because desire seeks more joy very naturally. Beginning from a place of frustration and suffering, too often, becomes a struggle with no end in sight. The briefest glimpse of bliss tells you that it exists, and then you can set your desires in motion to taste more joy, more bliss, more ecstasy. What better way for desire to achieve its true purpose of total fulfillment?

ACTIVATING THE SACRAL CHAKRA

This chakra strengthens every aspect of sensual life, but especially the connection between desire and your dharma, which supports the desires you need for your evolution and inner growth. A few things you can do apply to every chakra in general:

- Be in simple awareness. When you notice that you aren't, take a few minutes to center yourself.
- Meditate on the mantra *Vam* (page 84).
- Meditate on the centering thought "I am sensual" or "I embrace desire" (page 87).

Other steps are more specifically aimed at activating your power chakra. Beginning from a state of bliss, each desire is already primed to be fulfilled. This setup requires a shift in attitude, because, as things stand, desires arise from a sense of something missing.

The meditations for the second chakra show you how to experience desire as a generous overflow from "I am enough." Desires are meant to be an expansion of abundance, not a reaction to lack.

MEDITATION #1

Sit quietly, eyes closed, and take a few deep breaths until you feel centered. Now imagine an extravagant dream you wish would come true. It could be winning the lottery, finding a perfect romantic partner, sailing first class on a luxurious cruise ship—let your fantasy guide you.

Now envision in detail all the wonderful consequences of your fantasy. Use the other senses, too, if you can, such as hearing beautiful music. Sense the bliss that your fantasy brings. Let the bliss expand in your heart. Don't force anything. Even a hint of bliss is fine. After a few minutes, open your eyes, take a deep breath or two, and return to your regular activity.

The purpose of this meditation is to show you that your awareness is where bliss occurs. You need no outside trigger for gratification. Bliss is accessible simply by desiring it, using a fantasy as a subtle trigger.

MEDITATION #2

This is an advanced version of the first meditation. Sit quietly, eyes closed, and take a few deep breaths until you feel centered. Now smile inside. Don't trigger your smile using a fantasy, but simply bring the smile up because you desire it. You will probably find it helpful to smile on the outside first, then follow the impulse inside to the area of your heart.

Let your smile linger for a few minutes. If you get

distracted, easily return to your smile. The meditation is over whenever you feel that you sense a real smile inside. At any time you can open your eyes, take a deep breath or two, and return to your day.

This meditation accesses a blissful feeling directly, merely by desiring it. It is very useful to practice it several times a day. You are training your mind to recognize that it can have a blissful feeling at will. In time this will become second nature. If you have started the practice of centering yourself, anytime you feel that you have lost simple awareness, add a smile at the end. Feeling centered and calm, smile to yourself and let the blissful feeling suffuse your awareness.

MEDITATION #3

As you lie in bed just before falling asleep, review your day. Visualize each significant event. When you recall a good outcome, let the feeling of fulfillment linger. The event doesn't have to be a major success or achievement. It can be a kind word, a song you liked, or watching your children at play.

Whatever the image in your mind, let the blissful feeling around it sink in. This helps train your mind to pause and appreciate its access to bliss.

If you recall an unpleasant or unsuccessful event, let your negative feeling linger, as long as it isn't too troubling. If you find yourself getting upset all over again, open your eyes and take a few deep breaths. But if the event was a minor source of annoyance, worry, or sadness, let the feeling subside until it is gone. You can even say to the memory, "You have served me. I don't need you anymore." Also helpful is to breathe out the feeling with a steady stream of air through your mouth. In any case, you are asking the negative feeling to leave.

Once it has left, lie calmly for a moment, then return to feeling happy by smiling inside the way you did in the earlier meditation. This is a more advanced meditation than the others, because you are asking to transform negative emotions into positive ones. However, it is very worthwhile to master it, because once you can transform a negative feeling, it won't become lodged in your memory. Moreover, you will become more confident that you exist in a state of inner affluence, no matter what has befallen you during the day.

CHAKRA 1

Totally Grounded

FIRST CHAKRA

Location: Base of the spine

Theme: Connection with the Earth

Desirable qualities:

Grounded

Safe, secure, protected

Whole

The first chakra brings the journey of bliss-consciousness to its completion with a surprising twist. Bliss-consciousness is no longer confined to your mind and body. It now enters the physical world, reaching out-side to embrace everything around you. You feel completely at home, no matter where you are, because you are at home in yourself. Now there is no need to fear the world as being inherently risky, unsafe, or potentially dangerous.

This is a level of awareness that most of us would thankfully welcome since the twenty-four-hour news cycle keeps reinforcing over and over again the message that the world, in fact, is quite dangerous. A dramatic shift in perspective is possible, however, which creative intelligence can achieve for you.

The first chakra, located at the base of the spine, is commonly called the root chakra because all the higher chakras are rooted here. There must be a secure foundation before your life can soar. Traditionally, the first chakra represents grounding in the Earth, the physical world, but being grounded has several other implications. When we say that someone is grounded, we're describing a stable personality, down-to-earth and reli-able, not prone to flights of fancy.

Yoga teaches that when mind and body are in sync, you are grounded. The basic signs of being grounded include the following:

- You are comfortable in your body.

- You feel physically safe.

- You are not easily swayed by external influences.

- You welcome being here and now.

- You have stable biorhythms (including regular appetite and good sleep).

- You feel emotionally stable.

These are not qualities you set out to achieve on an agenda. They are the natural result of balance in the first chakra. Visualize bliss-consciousness flowing down from the crown chakra, moving down the spine, then down your legs into the ground. You are in perfect, dynamic balance when there is no obstacle along this whole pathway.

Grounding could be called first base in the game of life, but in this book I've saved it for last. The chakra system shows you how to live your life from the top down because the crown chakra is your source. As things stand, most people approach life from the bottom up, giving their material needs priority. The physical world provides, but it also takes away. Scarce resources, bad weather, economic hard times, and the struggle to survive are constant threats somewhere on the planet. Being prepared for threats produces anxiety and fear of losing what you have.

Nothing could be further from the teaching of Yoga, which places all needs, including survival needs, in consciousness rather than the physical world. You might object that food and shelter are too basic to be set aside in this way. If you think about it, however, you provide yourself with food, water, and shelter using your mind. You are not in the so-called state of nature. All animals and birds take care of their young until they are developed enough to fend for themselves. It's natural for them to do so. Only *Homo sapiens* extend the nurturing period well into adolescence and beyond because our development takes place in consciousness. The chakra system recognizes this and expands consciousness to its full potential.

Modern life has mostly lost this connection with the Earth. Restoring this connection can result in some dramatic experiences. I was given proof of this by Matthew, a friend who recounted to me one of his most life-changing experiences.

I came from a tough background with an alcoholic father and a sweet but passive mother. Looking back, I guess in today's jargon, she'd be called an enabler.

I got into meditation because I knew I had a lot of stored anger in me, and I could see happier people all around me. It was that simple, no great spiritual ambitions or anything. Somehow everything clicked for me. I became calmer inside and much less angry. Once I settled into the state of quiet mind, it grew in its appeal. I experienced what I thought was bliss.

One day, I was sitting to meditate, and within thirty seconds, a new, mild blissful feeling became very intense. This was new, I thought. Then a surge of love swept over me, and I distinctly felt that it was a mother's love. It came from inside me, not from remembering my mother. Being a man, it never occurred to me that I could feel maternal, but there it was—warm and feminine. The experience lasted no more than five minutes, but I really feel it changed me. I know for certain that the divine mother is real, because I experienced her touch.

Every spiritual tradition describes some form of divine mother, which hardly anyone acknowledges in the modern secular world. The seven chakras stand for the places inside us that we must explore to know who we really are. The first chakra tells you that you are a child of the Earth, and this realization is blissful—or it should be. One of the most damaging aspects of modern life is that we exploit the Earth without caring for it. A living entity, known as Mother Nature, has lost its mothering quality. This is a stark departure from thousands of years of tradition that centered spirituality around Nature as a source of abundance. Reconnecting with the Earth implies much more, then, than anyone might expect.

QUIZ

How Grounded Are You?

When you are connected with the Earth, your own physical nature is a source of bliss. Most people, however, have the opposite experience, judging against their bodies, fearing natural disasters, and believing that micro-organisms—the basic life-forms on the planet—are all "germs" that cause disease. Other people simply are not comfortably settled into the physicality of their bodies. To see what can result, consider ten basic questions:

1. Do you have a good body image?
   Yes ☐   No ☐

2. Do you like physical touching?
   Yes ☐   No ☐

3. Do you fall asleep easily and sleep well the whole night?
   Yes ☐   No ☐

4. Are you happy about your age?
   Yes ☐   No ☐

5. Do you feel that you have a healthy attitude toward sex?
   Yes ☐   No ☐

6. Do you enjoy being out in Nature?
   Yes ☐   No ☐

7. Do you find it easy to focus your mind whenever you want?

Yes ☐   No ☐

8. Do you have a long attention span?

Yes ☐   No ☐

9. Are you free of worry about your health in the future?

Yes ☐   No ☐

10. Do you enjoy physical activity?

Yes ☐   No ☐

If you answer "No" more than four times, you might not really be grounded in a balanced way. I am not casting blame or trying to alarm you. Modern life is increasingly sedentary and mental in the Western world. The opportunity to have physical activity is limited for millions of office workers, and the distractions that keep us on the couch or online mount all the time.

There are many lifestyle choices that can make a difference, both large and small, to reconnect you by strengthening the first chakra. Some will sound familiar, others might be new to you.

- Make sure you get good sleep, meaning eight to nine hours of continuous, uninterrupted sleep.
- Remain centered in simple awareness. As soon as you notice that you aren't centered, take a few minutes to center yourself.
- Make it a daily habit to practice a simple breath meditation, which consists of sitting quietly, eyes

closed, and easily following your breath for five to
ten minutes.

- If you spend long stretches sitting down at
  work or on your computer, get up once an hour,
  stretch, and move around for a few minutes.
- Find a means to have physical enjoyment that
  energizes your body, making sure that you don't
  turn exercise into work.
- If you begin to feel restless, agitated, distracted,
  or worried, nip that feeling in the bud. Don't
  delay, but return to a calm, centered state of
  awareness as soon as you can.
- Avoid conditions that throw off the involuntary
  nervous system. These include multitasking,
  frequent interruptions on the phone, loud noise
  levels, too many people asking for your attention,
  and a tense atmosphere. Look carefully at your
  immediate situation at home and work to see how
  many of these conditions can be improved.
- Get out in Nature for a relaxed walk and
  appreciate its beauty and tranquility.

"RIGHT REALITY"

Being grounded physically is essential, but the first chakra has more
to say. It brings spirituality literally down to Earth. In other words, higher
consciousness infuses physical reality.

What's at stake can be called "right reality." The acid test is whether your thoughts, feelings, sensations, desires, and intentions can alter physical reality. In the modern world, almost everyone—except for the religiously devout, who ascribe ultimate power to God—assumes that the counterargument is right. The physical world is the "right reality" by default because, from childhood onward, few of us have even heard the argument for consciousness.

The case for mind over matter is actually very strong, however. This strikes close to home every time you have a thought. To think a sentence like "The beach is filled with palm trees," the words must create brain activity, and this activity produces specialized molecules, known as neurotransmitters, that do not exist in the precise pattern you need until the thought occurs. Suppose you visualize those palm trees on a beach, see them swaying in the tropical breeze, or hear the lapping of ocean waves on the sand. In that case, each process is directed by the mind, with the brain obeying instructions by producing specific molecules suited to the task.

Mind over matter can be extended to extraordinary lengths. The world was startled in 2019 by the feats of a Tibetan Buddhist monk in Taiwan whose consciousness continued to control his body after death. The press report from the *Times of India* is worth quoting in full.

> *A Tibetan Buddhist scholar in Taiwan has entered into the rare spiritual meditative state of "thukdam" after being declared clinically dead on July 14, it has been claimed. Thukdam is a Buddhist phenomenon in which a realized master's consciousness remains in the body despite its physical death, the Central Tibetan Administration (CTA) said.*
>
> *Though they are declared clinically dead, their bodies show no signs of decay and are found to remain fresh for days or weeks without preservation. Scientific inquiry into this phenomenon had begun a few years ago under the initiative of Tibetan spiritual leader the Dalai Lama. After the clinical death of the Tibetan Buddhist scholar on*

July 14, the mortal remains of Geshe Gyatso were returned to his resi-
dence, the CTA's office in Taiwan said in a post. At the time, Taiwan
was in the midst of peak summer, yet nothing could be detected from
an observation of the mortal remains. The staff of the office of Tibet
revisited the body on the fifth day to determine signs of decay and de-
composition. Similarly, it was examined by medical professionals who
expressed their complete astonishment at the phenomenon.

The incorruptible nature of a saint's body after death has been well documented in Roman Catholicism. Still, it fell to Eastern traditions to create a meditation that enables a person's consciousness to achieve such powers, not by the grace of God but through regular practice. In the Taiwanese case, the Dalai Lama immediately ordered that neutral scientific observers be brought in to verify the phenomenon, which duly happened. The news report continues:

On July 24, the physicist [Yuan Tseh Lee] and his assistants from
Taiwan's research center, Academia Sinica, arrived and conducted
the first forensic examination on the monk . . . it revealed the blood
pressure of the body to be at 86, quite close to a living human, the
CTA said. Additionally, the suppleness of the skin, the apparently un-
decomposed state of the internal organs, the facial glow and warmth
was noted under close examination.

A doctor's examination showed significant brain activity, and skeptics might seize on this finding to argue that the monk wasn't actually dead. But brain death starts to occur within three minutes of the heart stopping, and, in this case, days went by with no cardiac activity.

In the tradition of Yoga, this affair would not be considered a miracle but an example of *siddhis*, the power of consciousness to extend into regions most people would call supernatural. While photos were taken to record that the Taiwan siddhi was real, we lack similar evidence for siddhis like bilocation, or being in two places at once (this is often attributed to Catholic saints, and it's sometimes cited by people claiming to send the fragrance of flowers into a distant place); living for decades or even centuries beyond a normal human life span (China has a long tradition of such Immortals, as they are called); or levitation (recorded anecdotally hundreds of times in the Indian and Catholic tradition).

A siddhi offers evidence that consciousness pervades matter, beginning with the human body. The domain of consciousness isn't "in here" or "out there," but both. Even this doesn't go far enough. Consciousness has no location. It is dimensionless, since you can't measure it in feet and inches, ounces and pounds, hours and minutes, here or there. This notion of being nowhere and everywhere at the same time is hard to grasp, I know. One approach, currently gaining popularity among physicists, is to see the whole universe as conscious. This is a far cry from the ironclad assumption that the universe is entirely physical and random.

But physics has been backed into a corner when it comes to consciousness. No one can prove, even remotely, that any combination of atoms and molecules can think, yet, obviously, we humans can. (We even think about thinking, which seems to be unique to our species.) Faced with the realization that physical processes cannot account for the emergence of mind, it became easier to jump to the conclusion that some kind of seed consciousness, or proto-consciousness, was part of creation from the beginning, like gravity.

BODY OF BLISS

We aren't concerned with cosmic questions here. I bring up the conscious universe only to show that modern science is beginning to agree with Yoga: Consciousness is basic. Yoga goes one step further by saying that consciousness is the real reality. It is quite remarkable that only one step is involved. Most people, including 99 percent of scientists, have a mental picture of life on Earth that begins with primitive one-celled organisms, like amoebas and blue-green algae. These hang around for a couple of billion years before multicelled organisms emerge, and then it takes another billion years to reach the age of the dinosaurs.

Yet mind is still hundreds of millions of years ahead in the future. If you assume that only human beings are conscious, our existence began only one or two million years ago. To bring this down to scale: If you measure the Earth's age as a single twenty-four-hour day, starting at midnight, primitive life begins to appear at six o'clock in the morning, multicelled organisms around noon, and our hominid ancestors in the last twenty seconds before the end of the day. This calculation is meaningless, however, if consciousness was built into creation. There would be no time period, however ancient, *without* consciousness.

Not only would consciousness always be present, but it would pervade atoms and molecules. Now you don't have to name when or where atoms and molecules learned to think. Thinking is happening no matter where you look, only it isn't human thinking in words and concepts. It is creative intelligence. The flow of creative intelligence becomes the very thing Darwinians call evolution, the big difference being that consciousness is evolving at the same time that physical traits are evolving. (A pure Darwinian, I hasten to add, sticks with physical traits. The evolution of consciousness has yet to find a new Darwin who will fit consciousness into the equation. Only Yoga has gotten there so far.)

If every atom and molecule in your body is part of the flow of creative intelligence, then so is every cell. When medical science, amazed at the immune system's intelligent activity, started calling the immune system a "floating brain," the door was open for seeing intelligence in cells that weren't confined to the enclosed space under the skull. We've already covered how the body manifests creative intelligence, but there's a bigger conclusion to draw, which is this: If your body expresses creative intelligence, you are inhabiting a body of bliss.

At moments of great joy and fulfillment, everyone feels a bodily reaction, such as tingling, lightness, or enhanced energy. We whoop and dance for joy because the body wants an outlet for its flood of bliss. Yet Yoga would point to the Tibetan Buddhist monk whose body survived death as a better example of the body of bliss. It was bliss-consciousness in his body that preserved it intact postmortem for the simple reason that, in life, consciousness keeps everyone's body intact in the first place.

In the Indian spiritual tradition, the body of bliss has a name: *Anandamaya kosha*, where *Ananda* is bliss and *Kosha* is body. We don't need to go into detail, but it is interesting that there is a system of Koshas that descends from the body of bliss to the body of thought, emotions, and, finally, the physical body. This journey is very similar to the journey of the seven chakras, in that the beginning is pure bliss-consciousness and the end point is physicality.

I've risked taking this discussion far from everyday life. If you've held on up to this point, however, you are on the verge of an astonishing "Aha!" You will realize that your consciousness and everything around you are one. The whole Earth is a body of bliss. There is no separation between the flow of creative intelligence in your body's atoms and molecules and the flow of creative intelligence in clouds, trees, amoebas, chimpanzees, and stars. You do not possess a mind surrounded by a physical world, where mindless matter rules. Consciousness is the invisible glue holding creation together at every level. This "Aha!" has enormous importance in daily life. For example:

- Your thoughts and desires are connected to the world "out there."

- Through this connection, you create the events around you.

- If you have an intention close to the source of bliss-consciousness, your intention will come true.

- At the source, your consciousness is exactly the same as cosmic consciousness.

Yoga teaches that there is a powerful connection between you and the universe that transcends the scope of the individual "I." By strengthening the first chakra, you start to inhabit a body of bliss that extends in all directions. Let's look more deeply into how this actually works.

THE *SHAKTI* CONNECTION

Your cosmic connection begins with everyday experiences and then extends into new territory. The simple fact that you can raise your arm by having a desire that travels through the central nervous system to your arm muscles is enough to prove that the mind-body connection is real. There is also an occasional experience of synchronicity, when you think something, and the next moment it manifests. A friend's name comes to mind, and she texts you a minute later. A random word comes to mind, and somebody says the word soon thereafter. (A friend gave me a striking example of synchronicity when he was a graduate student. Riding to a seminar on the bus, he had the word *praxis* come to mind. It wasn't a word he ever used, although he had taken Latin in high school and knew that this is the word for the practice of doing something. He arrived in class, the professor entered, and, before the seminar started, the professor wrote *praxis* on the blackboard, then turned to his students and announced that this would be the topic of the seminar that day.)

Synchronicity is defined as a meaningful coincidence, but there is no scientific explanation for it. You can attempt to explain a friend texting you by saying that one of you is psychic. Maybe my friend riding the bus might think he was psychic. The real issue is how a person's mind connects with the outside world. In Yoga, the explanation is a force called *Shakti* in Sanskrit, a word that has a whole range of connotations: energy, ability, strength, effort, power, and capability. If you have enough Shakti, your connection to the world is strong; without Shakti, you will exist somewhere between being helpless and living a life of struggle and setbacks.

Shakti applies to both mind and body. It takes Shakti to lift a heavy weight and also to multiply 43 times 89 in your head. But the Shakti we have focused on in this book is intelligent and creative; it powers events everywhere, from the big bang to the next breath you take. Shakti is cosmic. In Indian mythology, Shakti is the female consort of Shiva, forming the twin faces of creation—Shiva rules the invisible realm of all possibilities. At the same time, Shakti carries possibilities into the physical world. Her dance is the dance of creation.

When Shakti becomes personal, your body functions as it was designed to, with perfect correlation in every cell. You experience balance, health, and well-being as givens. When something starts to go out of balance or you experience poor health and a lack of well-being, Shakti has been impaired. There is no magic about restoring it. Simple awareness is all you need. Centered, calm, and quiet inside, you are giving Shakti an open channel once more. This is why, according to Yoga, meditation is good for the body. The beneficial effect that meditation has on blood pressure, heartbeat, immune response, and so on is that meditation puts you in simple awareness. (I'm not proposing a medical panacea. The most common lifestyle disorders in the modern world begin years, even decades, before symptoms appear. These causations are deeply entrenched, and in many cases meditation can do only so much. But this doesn't undermine the effectiveness that meditation is proven to have throughout mind and body.)

Now, every thought has Shakti, which means that thinking sends ripples of energy everywhere in creation. You are communicating to the physical world through the Shakti that you possess. Sometimes this is taken literally—an extraordinary person might rise from nowhere to become Jesus, Buddha, Napoleon, or Einstein because an unstoppable force pushes them forward. Yet Shakti isn't the force of destiny, nor is it like having more electricity in a power grid. Shakti exists to bring you everything you need to have—the same goal that bliss-consciousness always has.

As far as Yoga is concerned, everything in your life should be synchronous. If you think of someone's name and that person texts you, this should be a tiny step that benefits you. If you find a job you want, you should get it if it is right for your personal evolution. This is where conventional thinking breaks down. You might have heard the saying "Thank God for unanswered prayers." There are lots of things we think are good for us that turn out to be bad, and avoiding them is a blessing.

The gap in experiences is closed when what you want to happen is the very thing that *should* happen. So how do you get there? There are times when you feel that everything is going your way, nothing can stop you, and the world is wonderful. You are aligned with creative intelligence. But on other days you feel very out of sorts and have a difficult time. What makes the difference isn't an outside force, fate, or accident. The determining factor is your connection to, and alignment with, Shakti.

With my fellow MD and a brilliant thinker about consciousness, Anoop Kumar, we came up with three stages that tell you how strong your Shakti connection is. For simplicity's sake we call these Mind 1, 2, and 3.

Mind 1: You view life as a separate individual. The leading indicator of Mind 1 is the sense of being located in the body. As a result of being limited by the body, Mind 1 detects the physical world as separate. As we see ourselves, so we see the world. If you localize yourself in your body, you see a world of separate things that are not you. Other people live inside their own bodies, which gives them their own sense of separation. In Mind 1, you provide fertile ground for the ego. "I, me, and mine" become all-important. This makes perfect sense, because your agenda as a separate person is all about the experiences of pleasure and pain that the body feels. Even a mental state like anxiety is rooted in the body—what you fear comes down to a painful sensation "in here." In every re-spect, Mind 1 is dominated by yes and no to the experiences that come your way.

Mind 1 seems totally right and natural in the modern secular world. Mind 1 is reflected in science's total focus on physical things, from mi-crobes and subatomic particles, from the big bang to the multiverse. A best-selling book from 1970, *Our Bodies, Ourselves*, applies to all of us in Mind 1. The only Shakti you have is inside your body, just as your only identity is inside your body. This Shakti is very powerful—it holds every cell together—but it is also limited. Your state of awareness changes nothing in the outside world.

Mind 2: Mind 2 centers on the unity of mind and body. It isn't nec-essary to see yourself confined to a physical package of flesh and bones. In fact, this mind-set can be turned on its head. In place of isolation, there is connection; in place of things, there is process; in place of hard objects, there is a continuous flow. You relax into the flow of experience rather than slicing life into bits that must be judged, analyzed, accepted, or rejected.

Mind 2 lets you see yourself more clearly, because in reality the mind-body connection is a single whole. Every thought and feeling creates an effect in every cell. You can consciously create change in the whole system through an intention in awareness. Mind 2 is subtler than Mind 1—you have moved deeper inside who you really are, and your state of awareness becomes all-important. You are the one who experiences, observes, and knows.

For most people, Mind 2 begins to dawn when they meditate or do yoga, finding access to the quiet mind that lies beneath the surface of the restless active mind. With this discovery comes a way to see beyond the separate ego's fruitless search for "perfect" pleasure, power, or success. As a deeper vision of self and life soaks through all experience, Mind 2 is established. Just as important, you begin to see yourself reflected in the world. You realize that much of what has happened to you—good and bad—was influenced by your state of awareness. A life grounded in self-awareness is much better than one grounded in moods, whims, desires, prejudices, and fixed beliefs. Your connection with Shakti is in transition, no longer confined to your body but not yet powerful in the outside world.

Mind 3: Mind 3 expands awareness beyond all mind-made boundaries and radically changes what the word "I" means. Expanded awareness places you in an infinite field of creative intelligence, where all things exist as possibilities emerging through the power of Shakti. This is not only a clear view of your life, it is clarity itself, because there is no thing or process to obstruct your vision. Boundaries don't exist. There is no past or future. The clearest view you can possibly have is here and now.

When there are no boundaries to limit your vision, you are awake, which allows you to see things without any filter. Your past no longer holds you captive, and therefore you are free, which is why Mind 3 has been known for centuries as liberation. There are no more "mind-forg'd manacles," in William Blake's phrase. You can trust Shakti to support you spontaneously, just as your cells already do.

Mind 3 is open to everyone, but there is a large obstacle that must be overcome, which is this: We are convinced by the lens we see things through. Each mind-set feels real and complete. You identify with physical things in Mind 1, the most important thing being your body. In Mind 2 you identify with your field of awareness as it brings experiences and sensations that rise and fall.

Because it takes an inner journey to reach, Mind 3 isn't where the vast majority of humankind is, yet every experience of joy, love, compassion, beauty, peace, and self-awareness sets the ego aside, and for a moment you know that being awake is natural and very desirable. You go beyond "I" in a simple, natural glimpse of who you really are. You are the field of awareness itself, unbounded and free. Every possible experience originates here, before the filters of ego, society, family, school, and painful memories cloud your vision.

Mind 3 is the freedom you attain when you realize that you were meant to be free all along. Clear away the clutter, and freedom is simply there. Mind 1 and Mind 2 are creations, while Mind 3 is uncreated. The dance of Shakti is eternal, and when we join it, the inevitable feeling is that we've returned home at last. "I am enough" is your home from now on.

ACTIVATING THE ROOT CHAKRA

This chakra strengthens every aspect of being grounded, both physically and mentally. A few things you can do apply to every chakra in general:

- Be in simple awareness. When you notice that you aren't, take a few minutes to center yourself.
- Meditate on the mantra *Lam* (page 84).
- Meditate on the centering thought "I am always safe and secure" or "I am totally grounded" (page 87).

Other steps are more specifically aimed at activating the first chakra. We've covered the practice of centering yourself, which is basic to feeling at home in your body. Stress and distress throw you out of the grounded state. Exercise #1 is helpful in the same way.

EXERCISE #1

Sit quietly with both feet on the floor and your posture erect. Breathe in until your chest feels comfortably full. As you exhale, visualize a white beam of light traveling down your spine.

See the light split below the spine, going down each leg, through your feet, and into the Earth.

Repeat five to ten times. You don't need to repeat this on every breath, just whenever you feel ready. The grounding effect is helped along if you fold your hands in your lap and lower your shoulders. You are grounding your personal energy with the Earth, the source of life and belonging in the physical world.

EXERCISE #2

On a warm, sunny day find a clean patch of grass, preferably in a quiet spot in a park or in your backyard. Lie flat on your back, eyes closed. Spread your feet apart and lay your arms at your sides. Make sure this position feels comfortable.

Feel the weight of your body pulling you close to the Earth. Imagine that your body is getting so heavy that you feel no distance between you and the Earth.

Once you have this sensation, breathe deeply and comfortably. With each in-breath absorb the energy of the Earth coming up through the ground and suffusing your body. You can either feel this as a warm sensation or you can visualize golden light filling your body.

With each out-breath, simply relax and let the golden light and warmth settle in.

Repeat for five to twenty minutes, or whatever is comfortable for you.

OUR SPIRITUAL FUTURE TOGETHER

The themes of this book—Yoga, abundance, and creative intelligence—unfold on the page. But behind the scenes something else unfolded more darkly. I began writing when the pandemic had yet to grip the world and the book was finished after a lockdown lasting longer than anyone ever dreamed possible.

It's natural in troubled times for people to reflect on God as a source of solace and hope—our need for spiritual support spikes sharply in a crisis. This holds true even though Americans and Europeans have become less attached to organized denominations for decades. Like a winter coat that's put away in spring, for many people religion gets put away once the crisis has passed. But the need for spirituality doesn't pass like the seasons. This need is rooted more deeply than solace and hope. It's the need for wisdom. *Wisdom* is a word that's open to skepticism and dismissal. Even people who think of themselves as "spiritual" are likely to think much more about issues like self-esteem and love.

Wisdom is of crucial importance. It gives answers to why we exist and what our purpose is. In Yoga, wisdom offers a vision of consciousness itself, bridging all ages and circumstances. It gets at the heart of reality. Ultimately the search for reality is what binds the impulse in everyone to feel whole. Those who actually pause to listen to the silent voice of the true self are the fortunate ones in every age.

Yet no one can ever be abandoned by spirit, no matter whether they feel joy or despair. The poet Rabindranath Tagore makes this clear in a beautiful verse.

> Motes of dust dancing in the light
> That's our dance, too.
> We don't listen inside to hear the music—
> No matter.
> The dance goes on, and in the joy of the sun
> Is hiding a God.

This is an expression of hope eternal. Yet even though spirit abandons no one, the path to mature and lasting spirituality, to wisdom itself, begins when you listen to the music inside, as Tagore puts it, or to the magnetic attraction of the Self, as Yoga puts it.

Right now the search for wisdom is more important, I think, than the search for God. Ever since Aldous Huxley coined the phrase "the perennial philosophy," seekers in the West have come to realize that sectarianism is too narrow and religions too orthodox to contain the great body of wisdom that has accumulated over time. The spiritual scene unfolding around us is today's updated version of the perennial philosophy. It brings a smile to suppose that you can modernize the transcendent. It's really a kind of ploy, one that gets repeated generation after generation. You have to persuade people that higher consciousness is real. Fail to do that, and you will be preaching to the stones.

For many spiritual people, there's little doubt that organized religion is serving reactionary social forces and offering a dogmatic version of God. Yet it is far more deplorable to ignore the spiritual yearning that exists in us. The current spiritual scene may not fill the vacuum perfectly, but you can foresee the future of spirituality in what is happening today:

- People feel free to express themselves outside the doctrines of organized faiths.

- They feel open to experiences that earlier generations denied or condemned, and that arch-materialists totally deny.

- They are aware that spirituality is a broad river running back many centuries.

- They feel included in a magnificent human quest.

- They believe that evolution of consciousness is real and worth pursuing.

- They believe they can find a noble vision and begin to live up to it.

These things represent wisdom as personal experience, rather than words in a book, however sacred the text. Current spirituality embraces a huge number of people who have tasted transcendence in those moments when the veil of the ego-self drops away and reality is seen without interference by the ego, memory, and old conditioning.

From my own childhood I remember women gathering in my grandmother's house in Delhi, often accompanied by a wheezing little harmonium, and the voices of family and friends raised to praise God in the words of beloved mystical poets like Kabir and Mirabai. The verses express the purest yearning imaginable, as when Mirabai sings:

> Take me to that place where no one can go
>
> Where death is afraid
>
> And swans alight to play
>
> On the overflowing lake of love.
>
> There the faithful gather
>
> Ever true to their Lord.

Today, centuries later, the seekers one meets vary enormously: students and practitioners of yoga, meditators of every stripe, Jungians brought up in the fifties, freethinkers and flower children from the sixties, followers of teachers like J. Krishnamurti and gurus like Paramahansa Yogananda, and even Theosophists. The devout in organized religions radiate their own light and faith. It's a big tent.

Hopeful as the signs and portents are, this diverse movement is sometimes hard to decipher. Where are spirituality's successes in a troubled world? There don't seem to be many inroads into orthodox political or social thought. But as a grassroots movement, personal spirituality is powerful. We see it clearly in the unquenchable idealism of millions of people who either flirt with the appeal of wisdom or dive into it more deeply.

The path of wisdom, being timeless, is always open. I don't see an alternative, frankly, to our spiritual yearning. So whatever the spiritual scene morphs into thirty years from now, at this moment personal seeking and the inward path are the most viable movement we have, and it deserves to be considered on its own terms, without labels.

While pondering this epilogue, I thumbed through *The Soul in Love*, a book of poetry translations I was moved to write out of my passion for Rumi, Kabir, and Mirabai. Yoga is potent in its knowledge, but poetry sings to the heart. Wisdom needs no outward show, because nothing is happening outwardly. The soul's love is experienced when we go to an unchanging place beyond all worlds, blessed or troubled.

The future is an illusion born when the mind loses its timeless source. In that light, the voice of the timeless shows the path of wisdom. Rumi, as always, puts it with exquisite beauty:

> Only now and again do I suddenly sit up from my dreams to smell a strange fragrance. It comes on the south wind, a vague hint that makes me ache with longing, like the eager breath of summer wanting to be completed. I didn't know what was so near, or that it was mine—this perfect sweetness blossoming in the depths of my heart.

ACKNOWLEDGMENTS

This book has the unique feature of being written during the pandemic lockdown that began in the spring of 2020. That experience brought out two needs that deeply influenced my writing. First was the need for support. Let me express my gratitude for all the support that this project received no matter how physically isolated the circumstances became. As ever, I am deeply thankful for my editor Gary Jansen, who never wavers in his intelligent, perceptive partnership with me.

I am also grateful to acknowledge the support of everyone at Harmony Books, beginning with Diana Baroni—in today's book market, Diana has taken me through potential pitfalls and pointed out new opportunities with her keen insight and sharp decision-making. Thanks, too, to the whole Harmony team, including Tammy Blake, Christina Foxley, Marysarah Quinn, Patricia Shaw, Jessie Bright, Sarah Horgan, Michele Eniclerico, Heather Williamson, Jennifer Wang, and Anna Bauer.

The second need during the lockdown was the need to sustain the values that give life meaning and purpose despite setbacks in hard times. My sense of love and caring owes everything to my wife, Rita, and our extended family of children and grandchildren. Thank you for making this journey a shared venture that enriches all of us.

INDEX

Also by bestselling author
DEEPAK CHOPRA, MD

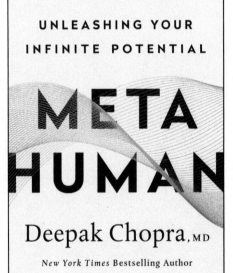

HARMONY
BOOKS · NEW YORK

Available wherever books are sold